1-10

Putting Off
ANGER

**A BIBLICAL STUDY of what anger is
and what to do about it.**

John Coblentz

Christian Light Publications, Inc.
Harrisonburg, VA 22802

PUTTING OFF ANGER

Christian Light Publications, Inc., Harrisonburg, Virginia 22802
© 1999 by Christian Light Publications, Inc.
Printed in the United States of America

5th Printing, 2009

Cover by David Miller

ISBN: 978-0-87813-579-0

CONTENTS

INTRODUCTION

"This know also, that in the last days perilous times shall come. For men shall be lovers of their own selves" (2 Timothy 3:1, 2). Where selfishness abounds, people get hurt. And where people get hurt due to selfishness, there is anger. That anger may come in a variety of forms—rage, frustration, resentment, or bitterness—and it may be expressed in a variety of ways—argument, violence, rejection, betrayal, screaming, name-calling, etc.

Anger, in its variety of forms and expressions, leads people into emotional bondage. There they live in prison cells of resentment and bitterness. Some prisoners want out. Some plot revenge. Some lose hope.

There is deliverance! When we are willing to take seriously the instructions of Jesus, we can find deliverance from the destructiveness of anger. Jesus came to break the bonds of sin and set captives free. Following Jesus' instructions cuts across the grain of our natural impulses. Following Jesus means rising above our feelings. But Jesus knows what He is talking about. He faced the very kinds of things that make people angry today—misunderstanding, mistreatment, hatred, violence, false accusation, betrayal, and rejection.

Anger is something everyone has to deal with, including this author. Many of the principles laid out in this book were learned in the heat of my own experience. I am grateful for the patience and goodness of God in His working with me and for His Holy Spirit who has often led me to my knees.

I am also grateful to the many people whose struggles

with anger drove me to seek God's answers for their particular strain of the anger virus, some of whose struggles are referred to in this book—names changed, of course, for their sakes and mine. In the process of listening to their problems and offering God's answers, I am certain I made mistakes. But I am grateful above all to God, who not only forgives our sins, but helps us correct our wrong ideas. His Word is timeless and unchanging, and I am still learning.

Human problems are far easier to define than to correct. This should not deter us from defining correctly, for proper definition helps us to know precisely what we are working with. The first three chapters of this book attempt to define anger and its wicked brother, bitterness. But we must go beyond simply describing our problems. The last four chapters offer solid Scriptural guidance for "putting off" anger and bitterness.

May the Lord's grace be with each one who reads this book with a sincere longing to be Christlike.

—John Coblentz

PART 1

Understanding Anger and Bitterness

CHAPTER 1

The Emotion of Anger

"I'd just as well tell you. You're looking at an angry, bitter man." Larry's dark eyes flashed and his body tensed, as he leaned against the door to leave. I had been talking to Larry for over an hour about his shaky marriage. Indeed, for months I had met repeatedly with Larry and his wife, and for a time we had made progress. But the situation had deteriorated again. Larry wanted desperately to save his marriage, but he was hurt and frustrated. And in his hurt and frustration he was contributing heavily, albeit sometimes unintentionally, to the deterioration. "The wrath of man worketh not the righteousness of God," the Apostle James wrote (1:20).

Countless wounds—physical, emotional, and spiritual— painfully attest to the truth of that Scripture. Anger kills people, turns children into rebels, disintegrates families, and divides churches.

Nobody disputes the destructive force of anger. Each of us has "anger stories" about ourselves or others, stories humorous or pathetic, about angry acts and the resulting damage. There are anger seminars, anger workbooks, anger therapists, and anger-control programs by the dozen. But their answers are nearly as diverse as the programs. The wide variety of solutions to this difficult human problem should hint strongly that we need more than "experts" to deal with it adequately.

The Word of God is not silent on the subject of anger. There are references to anger in one form or another in virtually every book of the Bible. To gain a Biblical understanding of this powerful emotion, and more importantly, to find help for controlling it, we will consider both prescriptive passages (where God tells us what to do or what not to do) and descriptive passages (where we will observe anger in action).

Why do people get angry?

We like to ask "why" questions. Sometimes why questions are merely attempts to shove off responsibility or to challenge authority. But in this case the question is asked to gain insights that will help us face and deal with the problem of anger.

1. *A person gets angry because he doesn't get his way.* King Ahab wanted Naboth's vineyard. When Naboth refused to trade or sell, Ahab went home "heavy and displeased. . . . And he laid him down upon his bed, and turned away his face, and would eat no bread" (1 Kings 21:4). We often see this in children. Their will gets crossed and they explode. But unfortunately, the problem is not limited to children, as Ahab aptly demonstrates. No matter what our age or status, when we don't get what we want, our natural response is anger.

2. *A person gets angry because things seem out of his control.* The more Saul lost control over David, the shorter his temper became. Praise for David shocked Saul's ego like an earthquake. The more Saul sought to eliminate David, the more miserably he failed, and Saul became

a very frustrated, angry man. Most of us will not readily identify with Saul—he is the bad person in the story. We identify with David. But under our masks, we are more often like Saul than we care to admit. When people do things that threaten our security or slight our ego, our efforts to counteract them seem only to result in more of the same.

A wife is trapped in a lifelong relationship with a man who seems oblivious to her. A minister wants desperately to have peace in his church, but certain troublemakers refuse to cooperate. Frustration over situations and people we cannot change eats in us like a cancer.

3. *A person gets angry to control.* This is only an extension of the former reason. Saul, like many of us, learned that anger makes people back off and often give in. It even makes some people willing to cater to you. A loud voice, a fist on the table, a lethal glare keeps others hopping. Anger controls. Rather than face the difficulty of confrontation with an angry person, most people bend. The ironic result, however, is more insecurity. Control gained through anger is generally good only as long as the controller is around. Nobody really respects the person who controls through intimidation. But anger, like most other emotions, doesn't have much foresight. It is focused on the immediate situation.

4. *A person gets angry in response to hurt or mistreatment.* When David and his men were rebuffed by Nabal, David put on his sword and set out to annihilate the whole Nabalite "tribe." David's reaction was typical. Sharp, sudden pain easily triggers curses and unleashes blind rage. And it matters little if the pain is physical or emotional. Vengeful anger may also grow little by little over years of mistreatment. And

once a wound is open, the angry person may become extremely touchy. Slight mistreatment, even words or actions not at all intended to hurt, may trigger angry reaction.

5. *A person gets angry because his pride is wounded.* The Bible records that King Asa faced a horde of invading Ethiopians that outnumbered the Israelite army two to one. Asa humbly and fervently sought the Lord. God not only gave him a tremendous victory, but also brought a great revival among the Israelites—many from the northern tribes went over to Asa "when they saw that the LORD his God was with him" (2 Chronicles 15:9). Shortly after this, however, and perhaps in retaliation for the political fallout, Baasha, king of the northern tribes, came against Asa. This time Asa sent a "league payment" to the Syrian king Ben-hadad to get him to break off his agreement with Baasha and form a union with Asa instead. It worked. But Hanani, a prophet of God, rebuked Asa for relying on a heathen king instead of relying on the Lord. Asa's response? "Then Asa was wroth with the seer, and put him in a prison house; for he was in a rage with him because of this thing. And Asa oppressed some of the people the same time" (2 Chronicles 16:10).

How could Asa switch so rapidly from urging people to follow the Lord to lashing out at the godly? Someone touched his ego, that's why. That Asa's pride was founded on his spiritual progress made it all the more subtle. Out of wounded pride a minister may make an angry reply to a just criticism, or a father may lash out at children who see through his mistake. Wounded pride hurts.

6. *A person may get angry as a spillover from unresolved guilt.*

David was guilty of immorality and covered-up murder. When he was told a story about a rich man who took advantage of a poor man, however, he exploded. Covered sin makes us touchy. A man who secretly looks at pornography or attends peep shows on the sly will almost invariably be harsh with his children. A person who lives with a burdened conscience often wields a criticizing tongue. Such a person is continually engaged in the subconscious task of trying to transfer his guilt to someone else.

7. *People also get angry in order to set wrong things right.* We all have a sense of justice. When David heard about the rich man taking his poor neighbor's only sheep to feed unexpected guests, David was incensed. Rightly so. There is a righteousness in this kind of anger. When a situation is wrong, anger is a motivation to set things right. Moses saw the lewdness of the calf-worshiping Israelites and was furious. Jesus saw the irreverence of the moneychangers in the temple and took decisive action. When we see two big boys beating up on a little boy, we have the same emotional response. We call it righteous indignation, and it is.

But there is a very subtle catch to this last kind of anger. Because it stems from our sense of justice, it feels right. It is JUSTIFIABLE. And without further thought, we easily make two mistakes. First, we transfer the rightness of our anger to whatever action we choose to take. Anger, like dynamite, is extremely explosive. Action powered by anger can cause terrible destruction. So the "Be ye angry" of Ephesians 4:26 is strictly limited with the imperative, "SIN NOT!" Being right in our assessment of a wrong situation does not mean we are right in using any means to set that situation straight. Although the anger may be justified, the action motivated by that "righteous anger" may be more wrong, more destructive, and more wicked in its hate and vengeance than the original injustice that stirred our anger. What can begin, in other words, as a right judgment that something is wrong can turn quickly into unrighteous passion to do even worse. Wars erupt out of this kind of righteous anger. Once the fuse is lit, the most heinous crimes are committed to "make wrongs right."

The second mistake we easily make under the halo of righteous indignation is considering all our anger to be righteous. No matter what stirs our anger, our mental processors make it out to be a wrong of some sort. Maybe we didn't get our way, our pride may have been wounded, we may be touchy as a result of carrying unresolved guilt, but in our minds we turn the episode into a wrong that needs to be made right. A young man is not allowed to go with his friends, and mentally he turns it into an injustice. An inconsistency is pointed out to a minister. Immediately he balances this against all the good he has done and the sacrifices he has made, and he feels terribly misunderstood.

Again, once the anger seems justified, so do the words and actions that follow. The young man slams the door of his room and shuts himself in for the evening. The minister says, "If that's all you think of my hard work for this congregation these past ten years, I'll go somewhere else."

As we can see, anger wells up for a variety of reasons. And if we glance over the Biblical examples, we can see also that anger takes a variety of forms. It may be an explosive temper, a seething rage, a pout, a sob story, or a long-term, low-burning resentment. Or it may be a zeal that cries out for appropriate action.

Understanding Anger

"Be ye angry, and sin not: let not the sun go down upon your wrath: Neither give place to the devil.... Let all bitterness, and wrath, and anger, and clamour, and evil speaking, be put away from you, with all malice" (Ephesians 4:26, 27, 31).

How do we understand what appears to be instruction to be angry followed so closely with the command to "put off" anger? As we have seen, righteous people sometimes become angry (e.g. Moses, David, Jesus, etc.). But righteous people cannot be called angry people. They are, in fact, distinct for their meekness, or control, under provocation.

To further understand anger, consider these points:

1. *Anger is an emotion.* When we get angry, we feel something deep within us. Physically, a chemical reaction takes place in our brain cells which triggers a release of adrenaline, pumping more blood to the brain and increasing heart rate and blood pressure. Depending on the intensity and focus of our anger, we may or may not be aware of these physical responses. But we are distinctly aware of how we feel deep inside.

   We can mentally categorize our emotions into roughly two groups: what we like and what we don't like. We like to feel happy, safe, loved, needed, pleasantly surprised, relaxed, trustful, friendly, etc. We don't like to feel threatened, anxious, angry, disappointed, panicky, used, betrayed, or embarrassed.

   Viewing anger as an emotion helps us understand it. Anger is part of human experience. It fits into the range of feelings affecting who we are, how we interact with others, and how we respond to life's problems and challenges.

2. *As an emotion, anger is to some extent involuntary.* We must distinguish here between anger as a feeling and anger as action. In our day-to-day speech (and often in Biblical usage) no such distinction is made. When we say "He has a terrible anger problem," we are usually referring to the expression, not the feeling, of anger.

Likewise, when the Bible tells us to put off anger, perhaps the primary emphasis is not so much forbidding any feeling of anger (although godliness certainly restrains feelings at times), but rather, forbidding those destructive words and actions provoked by anger.

As an emotion, anger is not primarily a choice. Although we may at times choose not to be angry about something or we may choose to cease being angry, and we certainly make choices about what to do when we feel angry, the initial feeling is not a matter of decision. The Biblical command, "Be ye angry, and sin not" (Ephesians 4:26) has been interpreted in various ways, usually with the force of the imperative rightly on the latter half—"sin not." Thus, some translations render this, "In your anger," or "When angry," conveying the assumption that anger is part of our experience. Sometimes we will feel angry, in other words, and often we will feel justified in feeling angry, but we must NOT sin. With this emphasis, "Be ye angry, and sin not" is better understood as a single command than as two separate commands.

3. *Emotions are reflectors.* One writer referred to emotions as reflectors. Though certainly more than that, our emotions do reflect our situations. Part of being human is to respond emotionally to what is going on around us. This makes life meaningful, colorful, and real to our senses. When a loving husband emerges from a jet walkway after two weeks away from home, his family not only knows he is returning, but they feel longing, love, gladness, inquisitiveness, excitement, and security in the reunion with him. Have they chosen these emotions? Certainly not. Their emotions involuntarily reflect their situation. And

imagine at that moment an announcement comes over the PA system to evacuate the airport immediately because of a bomb threat. Will they choose to feel tense or afraid? Or would they consciously choose to retain their former feelings because they like those feelings better? The point is that our emotions reflect our circumstances.

Emotions reflect more than circumstances, however. Included in the reflecting process is the person himself. Differences in people result in differences in emotional reflections. A situation that amuses one person may disgust another. If a big boy threatens a little boy, the little boy may feel fear, but an adult hearing the same threat may feel indignant.

Because character plays a part in emotional reflection, and choices form character, we must emphasize again, emotional responses are not totally involuntary. To the extent we are responsible for the kind of person we have become, we are also responsible for our emotional responses to situations. The goal of every Christian should be to become like Christ. This is primarily to bring glory to God; but the emotional result of Christlikeness is that in any situation, our feelings will be what Christ's own would have been in just such a situation. What would make Him happy, will make us happy. What would disgust Him, will disgust us.

Therefore, if I am angered where Jesus would not have been angered, something in my life needs changing. I must not use the logic, "I just couldn't help myself," to justify my anger. Rather, I must acknowledge that my temper (or resentment or self-pity or vengeance) reflects un-Christlikeness in my life. I must accept responsibility for my anger as well as for my need of change.

4. *Anger is a powerful emotion.* Emotions not only reflect our circumstances but urge responses to our circumstances. Some emotions particularly urge action. Anger is one of the most powerful emotions. In the Bible, one of the primary measures of a person's strength is the ability to control this powerful emotion. "He that is slow to anger is better than the mighty; and he that ruleth his spirit [controls his temper, NIV] than he that taketh a city" (Proverbs 16:32).

5. *Uncontrolled anger is destructive.* We have already noted Biblical examples of anger's destructive power. Anger has been the motivation behind the most terrible acts in history. Daily the papers are filled with the results of uncontrolled anger—a policeman is shot, a suicide bomber kills an entire busload of people, a child suffers permanent brain damage from a beating. But underneath and behind that physical destruction is emotional destruction just as horrible. Grief, terror, anxiety, bitterness, loneliness, despair, and inferiority fester and ooze like open sores on the soul and spirit.

The destructive effects of anger are not limited to those stung by outbursts of angry words and actions. Anger's destruction is inward also. In fact, terrible as the outward effects are, the inward effects on the angry person himself are worse. An angry person destroys himself. The destruction is the more terrible because it is not obvious. Frederick Beuchner wrote, "Of all the seven deadly sins, anger is probably the most fun. To lick your wounds, smack your lips over grievances long past, roll over your tongue the prospect of bitter confrontations still to come, savor to the last toothsome morsel both the pain you are given and the pain you are giving back—is a feast fit for a king. The chief drawback is that what you are wolfing down is yourself. The skeleton at the feast is you."

Study Questions (Chapter One)

1. Reflecting on the material in this chapter, finish this statement in as many ways as you can: Anger is _____.

2. What are some of the visible indications of anger?

3. Of the seven reasons given why people get angry, which do you think is most common?

4. Which of the seven do you personally struggle with the most?

5. Anger has different forms. With the help of a dictionary, define the following forms of anger:
   a. temper tantrum
   b. rage
   c. frustration
   d. irritation
   e. pouting
   f. resentment
   g. bitterness

6. How do the above forms of anger relate to the different causes of anger described in this chapter? (For example, which forms of anger would be common when a person is mistreated?)

7. In your own words, describe the two mistaken ideas we can easily have about "righteous indignation."

8. Read about Cain's anger in Genesis 4. Explain how he made both of the above mistakes in his thinking.

9. Explain how it is both right and wrong to view anger as involuntary.

10. For each of the following characters, describe what you think was his/her emotional response to Jesus' Crucifixion:
    a. the soldiers
    b. the religious leaders
    c. Jesus' mother
    d. the centurion
    e. Pilate
    f. someone Jesus had healed

11. Which of the above would you suppose may have struggled most with anger as a response? Explain your answer.

12. How do differences in people's character explain differences in their emotional responses to a given situation?

13. After studying this chapter, why do you think God made us with the capacity to get angry?

14. List some of the destructive effects of an uncontrolled temper.

15. What does control of one's temper indicate about one's character? (See Proverbs 16:32.)

CHAPTER 2

THE ROOT OF BITTERNESS

Around town, Bill was as jolly as sunshine. His face had so many smile crinkles that nobody thought about whether or not he was good-looking. He was just Bill, and people liked him. But most of Bill's children needed counseling to work through the emotional wounds received as Bill's children.

Bill was supersensitive. When he felt hurt or threatened, he lashed out verbally. Judgmental conclusions fell like sledge hammer blows. Events from the past were dredged up and flung like rotten tomatoes in people's faces. Bill was not a good communicator, but when he became upset, the home atmosphere was thick with dire predictions and emotionally charged accusations.

The roots of Bill's anger went back to his own childhood. Other boys often made fun of him and took advantage of his small size. His parents were not close to him, and Bill learned to keep his hurts to himself. He covered them over with an exterior cheerfulness, but inwardly he felt inferior and often dressed his wounds with self-pity.

The Bible says, "Follow peace with all men, and holiness, without which no man shall see the Lord: Looking diligently lest any man fail of the grace of God; lest any root of bitterness springing up trouble you, and thereby many be defiled" (Hebrews 12:14, 15).

In these verses, bitterness is referred to as a root. It is an apt description because bitterness works underground, as it were. Bitterness typically has been growing for some time before anyone sees it "springing up."

But notice two effects of bitterness once it sprouts: First, it brings trouble to the bitter person. There are few human problems with more severe personal consequences. Bitterness eats at the soul, sours the spirit, and poisons the body. The second consequence of bitterness is that it defiles others. Bitterness wrecks friendships, divides families, and tears apart churches. In its wake are many hurting people. Some are bitter in their turn. Some are confused. Some, by the grace of God, may rise above their hurt. But the interpersonal consequences of bitterness are many and evil.

Bitterness begins with a bitter experience.

In the Bible numerous kinds of experiences are referred to as "bitter." The Hebrew word conveys the literal meaning of "sharp tasting, or extremely sour." A bitter experience, then, is one that causes a natural reaction of distaste. If it were possible to spit out the experience, that is what we would do.

Notice the uses of the word *bitter* in the following verses:

1. "And when Esau heard the words of his father, he cried with a great and exceeding bitter cry, and said unto his father, Bless me, even me also, O my father" (Genesis 27:34). Esau was bitter because he felt cheated. And perhaps adding to this was the parental favoritism at work behind the scenes.

2. "And the Egyptians made the children of Israel to serve with rigour: And they made their lives bitter with hard bondage, in mortar, and in brick, and in all manner of service in the field: all their service,

wherein they made them serve, was with rigour" (Exodus 1:13, 14). The Israelites tasted the bitter experience of oppression—powerful people taking advantage of them and keeping them in economic and material straits.

3. "But unto Hannah he gave a worthy portion; for he loved Hannah: but the LORD had shut up her womb. And her adversary also provoked her sore, for to make her fret, because the LORD had shut up her womb. . . . And she was in bitterness of soul, and prayed unto the LORD, and wept sore" (1 Samuel 1:5, 6, 10). Hannah faced the bitterness of being a barren woman, but her bitterness was heightened by feminine competition with her rival wife. The taunting of Peninnah rubbed salt into an already festering sore.

4. "Then Abner called to Joab, and said, Shall the sword devour for ever? knowest thou not that it will be bitterness in the latter end?" (2 Samuel 2:26). A battle was raging between fellow Israelite armies. Abner, at whose urging the battle had begun, now had the foresight to see the bitter consequences if it continued. "Infighting" (quarreling within one's own group) whether in a country, a community, a congregation, or a family, is a bitter experience. There are far too many Abners who form battle lines, setting brother against brother, and far too few Abners who blow the trumpet and say, "Enough of this!"

5. "My flesh is clothed with worms and clods of dust; my skin is broken, and become loathsome . . . Therefore I will not refrain my mouth; I will speak in the anguish of my spirit; I will complain in the bitterness of my soul" (Job 7:5, 11). Physical suffering, weakness, and chronic pain wear on emotional nerves as acutely as on physical nerves. Job took his terrible

losses without a murmur against God, but unrelenting pain brought from him bitter complaint. Although Job never denied God, he certainly lost sight of Him behind the dark cloud of physical suffering.

6. "A foolish son is a grief to his father, and bitterness to her that bare him" (Proverbs 17:25). Only those Christian parents who have had a wayward child can know the anguish that gnaws at the heart, driving sleep from the eyes and joy from the spirit. Seeing a son or daughter walk away from all he has been taught is a bitter pill that refuses to go down.

7. "And I find more bitter than death the woman, whose heart is snares and nets, and her hands as bands" (Ecclesiastes 7:26). Solomon knew the bitterness of idol-worshiping women who pulled at him to do their will. Having a manipulating, controlling companion, whether wife or husband, is a source of bitterness.

8. "Thus saith the LORD; A voice was heard in Ramah, lamentation, and bitter weeping; Rahel [Rachel] weeping for her children refused to be comforted for her children, because they were not" (Jeremiah 31:15). Death of a little one, death of a parent, death of a companion—death of anyone close to us—is a bitter experience. The finality of no more earthly relationship, the manner of dying, and sometimes the nature of the relationship mingle in this bitter cup of death and grief.

To the above bitter experiences, we might add the bitterness of rejection, the bitterness of abuse, the bitterness of betrayal, the bitterness of terminal illness, and the list could go on of bitter experiences life brings.

As we see in the above examples, however, people can and do respond differently to these bitter experiences.

Furthermore, although nobody experiences all of these experiences, everyone can identify with some bitter experience. The reality is harsh but true: nobody can go through life without pain.

The stinging experience of pain, injustice, or death turns some people into cynics. Many are the poems, novels, and essays that smear life with blackness and gloom.

The Bible, as we noted above, does not ignore these dark realities. Nor does it promise that God's children will be spared from them. In fact, Job's suffering seems more poignant in its confusion because of his faith in God. What, then, are the answers? How do we cope with these bitter experiences?

Before we answer that, we need to look more deeply into the response chosen by too many that is NOT the correct answer. The natural emotional response to a bitter experience is bitterness. It is so natural, so "logical," and so subtle in its wrongness that we need to examine it in detail.

Bitterness grows out of anger.

"Be ye angry, and sin not: let not the sun go down upon your wrath: Neither give place to the devil" (Ephesians 4:26, 27). The immediate danger of anger is to sin. That is, we are apt on the spur of the moment to violate the ways of God. But there is another danger, equally real, and that is to hang on to our anger. The danger of hanging on to anger is that we may give a "place" (literally a foothold) for the devil to work.

Food left over from one day to the next (and the next and the next) changes form. It spoils, begins to stink, and draws flies which breed maggots; we call it garbage. Anger goes through a process no less nauseous when carried around in a person's heart. It, too, changes form. Anger sours into resentment, internal murmuring, blame patterns, self-pity, frustration, and discouragement. Bitterness sets in.

Unfortunately, the spoilage and stink are far more appar-ent and offensive to those around the embittered person than to the person himself. As with bad breath—everyone can smell it except the one who has it.

How does this process work?

1. *Bitterness often begins with a bitter experience.* It may be any one of the experiences we considered from the lives of Biblical characters, or it may be something differ-ent. But bitter people usually have some point of pain in their past.

2. *The bitter experience stirs deep emotional responses.* We feel deeply when we go through these bitter experiences—our feelings are reflecting our circumstances. We feel the bitterness of rejection, injustice, loss, grief, or abuse. The memories of a particularly bitter event may be burned into our minds, as it were, leaving a permanent mark. Or the injustice may not be a one-time event in the past, but an ongoing reality we face every day. In either case, to avoid letting "the sun go down" upon our anger may seem as impossible as making the sun stand still. The feelings are there because the situation is real.

   How does one dismiss the frustration of regularly being called an idiot (or worse) by someone who is supposed to love you? Or how does one dismiss the soul-sapping rage and revulsion of betrayal by a marriage partner?

3. *Anger (in all its forms) urges verbal and behavioral responses.* Spur-of-the-moment anger often urges an immediate lashing out. Anger carried over from one day to the next begins immediately to change form. It is turning into resentment. And although resentment does not feel exactly like the initial anger, it nonetheless provokes certain behavioral and verbal responses.

Resentment urges us to mentally review the painful experience, roll the injustice of it around in our mind, and think of the "price" the offender ought to pay. This mental process expresses itself directly or indirectly in our speech and actions. Resentful people complain, criticize, or curse those who mistreat them. They plot revenge. Others avoid direct expression, but the inner resentment sours their attitude toward the offender.

4. *The resentment settles into bitterness.* Bitterness is essentially a pattern of blame. A bitter person inwardly (and often outwardly) points an accusing finger at others, holding them accountable for what the embittered one is facing. Unfortunately, others may have caused suffering. Bitterness, however, makes the offender the continual mental companion of the bitter person. The offender is carried with him into his work, into his recreation, into his sleep, even into his worship. Everywhere the bitter one goes, he is accompanied by the offender and the offender's ugly words and actions.

The most subtle aspect of the anger process is that the longer it is held onto, the more natural and reasonable and "right" it seems to be. But though it is seeming more right, it is becoming more deadly.

Bitterness has various stages.

We have already looked at how bitterness forms out of anger. We know bitterness is progressive. But let's examine more closely the stages of bitterness itself.

1. *The hurting stage.* In one sense, this may not be a stage of bitterness, but inasmuch as all bitterness stems from hurt feelings, we will include it here. This is the

stage where we feel pain. When we have been mistreated, or when we have had some other painful experience, we hurt. It is not necessarily wrong to hurt. In fact, it is no less normal to feel emotional pain from mistreatment than to feel physical pain.

When the women of Israel came out of the cities praising David more than Saul, Saul was both hurt and angry. They sang, "Saul hath slain his thousands, and David his ten thousands" (1 Samuel 18:7). When Saul heard this, the saying "galled him" (NIV). Without justifying Saul's anger, we can say the women's public comparison of the two men was thoughtless and insensitive.

On the other hand, we must recognize sometimes we feel hurt when we ought not to. Once bitterness took over in Saul's life, he became hurt and angry even when others meant him well. He killed Ahimelech, for example, and the priests with him because Ahimelech had innocently given David food.

Emotional pain is a normal response to hurt, but some hurt is of our own making. All emotional pain is potential for bitterness, but that of our own making is inevitably so.

2. *The festering stage.* This is the stage of mental review. It is the time spent in the days, weeks, and months following my hurt, mentally going over what happened, what was said, and who did what and where and when and why. In this stage, I continue to feel pain, but I am also feeding my resentment by continually pressing my mind's replay button. Often the hurt person gets weary of the mental process and tries to think of something else. Apart from God's grace, however, this is nearly impossible. Those who do manage to shut out the mental misery-go-round

usually do so by using conscious or subconscious strategies of denial or repression. These strategies may seem to arrest the bitterness process, but in actuality only bury it and eventually cause other problems.

To an emotional hurt, mental review is the equivalent of a wounded person unceasingly unwrapping the bandage on a physical wound, looking at the wound, and replacing the bandage. It doesn't allow healing to take place.

3. *The collecting stage.* As resentment is fed through mentally reviewing the hurt, an unconscious desire develops for more hurt. No bitter person would admit it, but there is something gratifying about learning that an offender has "done it again." The dangers of this stage of bitterness are several. The bitter person actually begins looking for hurts and secretly finds gratification in receiving them. This sets up the bitter person for interpersonal trouble, not only with the one(s) whom he blames, but also with his friends. As he learns to accumulate grievances, he unknowingly accumulates social habits and attitudes that affect all his relationships.

4. *The self-pity stage.* This stage proceeds naturally from the former one. As people become bitter, they view themselves more and more as victims. In their conversations with others, this victim mentality comes to dominate everything they do and everything done to them. All humans struggle with accepting personal responsibility for certain kinds of behavior. We all at times want to point the finger and shift the blame. With a bitter person, however, this problem is amplified. All of life comes to be viewed through the darkened lenses labeled, "Not my fault," or "Look

what he did," or "People treat me terribly." Sympathy is soaked up like water.

Ironically, the more pity a bitter person seeks, the less he finds. The slightest injury sends the self-pitying person into the "poor me" mode—sighs, tears, silent suffering, and whining. The tendency of those observing this pity party is at best to politely ignore the person, and at worst, to react in disgust. We will look later at how to respond to a bitter person, but both sympathy and disgust are harmful responses.

5. *The stubborn stage.* The further bitterness progresses, the more entrenched it becomes. Bitter people come to the place where they refuse to let go of their anger, their blame patterns, and their self-pity. It has become their security. They guard their sore spots jealously. Wounds are their way of life, trials are their way of thinking, pouting and shifting the blame are their way of relating to others.

A bitter person holds tenaciously to his bitter feelings and his bitter outlook. He falls into that ironic emotional bondage where he is not happy unless he is miserable about something. Those around him may wish to help him out of his misery. But the more they try, the more offended he becomes. A bitter person will become so bound in blame patterns that the most loving words and actions of those around him are turned into wounds.

The subtlety of bitterness is that the stubbornness is two-way. The more a bitter person hangs onto his bitterness, the more bitterness sinks its claws into the bitter person. The bitter person increasingly comes under the control of bitterness, so that he cannot shake it off even if he wants to.

We might note here that the Apostle Paul warned against day-old anger. If anger carried over to the next day is spiritually dangerous, offering the devil a foothold, what about week-old anger? Or month-old? Or year-old? Some people have patterns of blame associated with specific people that go back 20, 30, or 40 years. With such bitterness, the devil's foothold becomes a fortress, complete with a dungeon and a torture chamber.

This is not saying there is no hope for a bitter person. It is saying bitterness can lead to a demonic bondage from which the only deliverance is in the Lord Jesus, who was "manifested, that he might destroy the works of the devil" (1 John 3:8). Paul tells Timothy to be gentle, patient, and meek in approaching those who have fallen under the "snare of the devil, who are taken captive by him at his will" (2 Timothy 2:26).

Study Questions (Chapter Two)

1. Make a list of the bitter experiences referred to in the first section of this chapter (including the ones mentioned at the end of the list). Then pick out two or three that would seem most difficult to you. Why do you think they would be difficult?

2. Which of the bitter experiences have you personally experienced? What have you experienced that was not listed?

3. Some people experience more pain and difficulty in life than others do. How does this fact test our faith?

4. This chapter has a section showing how bitterness grows out of anger. The Bible says Esau became bitter. Trace the progression from anger to bitterness in Esau's life, beginning with the account at the end of Genesis 25 and continuing through the next chapters.

5. What might Esau have done to avoid becoming bitter?

6. What are some evidences of bitterness in a person's life?

7. How does bitterness damage the bitter person?

8. List the stages of bitterness given in this chapter and give a one-sentence description of each stage.

9. In Chapter One, we looked at anger as an involuntary emotional response. Bitterness sets in after there has been more time to think. List some of the mental processes associated with the stages of bitterness.

10. To what extent might the difference between anger and bitterness (an emotional response vs. mental processes) explain why bitter people often do not believe they are bitter?

11. What is our typical response to a person seeking pity?

12. How can our relationship to the pity-seekers affect our response to them?

13. List a number of reasons people become "stubbornly bitter."

14. What are the dangers of hanging onto bitterness?

CHAPTER 3

THE DECEITFULNESS OF ANGER AND BITTERNESS

A nger in all its forms is dangerous. It is capable of terrible destruction, not only for those on the receiving end, but also for the angry one. Anger is also deceptive. It twists thinking, distorts perspective, and plays games with truth. The Apostle John addressed this very point. "He that hateth his brother is in darkness, and walketh in darkness, and knoweth not whither he goeth, because that darkness hath blinded his eyes" (1 John 2:11).

Everyone will feel anger. It is part of being human. Taking Ephesians 4:26 as it reads, we can also say anger is part of being Christian. Some situations and people will stir us to anger—even *should* stir us to anger. But when we are angry, we are warned immediately not to sin, and warned further not to carry our anger with us: "Let not the sun go down upon your wrath." A few verses later, we are commanded, "Let all bitterness, and wrath, and anger, and clamour, and evil speaking, be put away from you, with all malice" (v. 31).

The moment we feel anger, we are in danger of sinning. But when we allow anger to take up residence in our heart, sin is inevitable. Along with this sin goes deception. Resident anger distorts perspective. It causes us to make distorted assumptions, see with a distorted perspective, and draw distorted conclusions.

To unmask the deceitfulness of anger, we will look closely at an angry man in the Bible. King Saul did not start out as an angry man. In fact, his beginning seems to be characterized by a remarkable humility and depth of character. But once anger took up residence in Saul, it twisted his thinking and turned him into a bitter, domineering, hostile leader.

How anger developed in Saul.

Saul's sad story is told in 1 Samuel. To understand the deception that occurred, note the events in Saul's life that led to his anger and bitterness.

1. Saul was chosen to be Israel's first king. This position was given to him by God. It was not something Saul sought or won by campaign. In fact, after he was anointed king in a private ceremony away from home, he did not even mention it to his family; and on the day of his public coronation, he had to be flushed out of hiding to receive the crown.

2. Saul faced pressures as Israel's first king. He was scorned as king by some of the Israelites—a situation he handled humbly and commendably. He also faced the pressure of invading armies.

3. Saul was commissioned by God to destroy the Amalekites totally, but he did not carry out God's directions. God consequently told Saul he was rejected as king and another would take his place who would obey God.

4. In a private ceremony and unknown to Saul, Samuel anointed David to be the next king of Israel.

5. The Spirit of God departed from Saul, and he was tormented by an evil spirit. Saul's servants recommended that he get someone skillful in music to play

for him and relieve his bad moods. David was chosen, and his playing on the harp made Saul feel better.

6. Saul and his armies faced a challenge from the Philistines. The giant Goliath challenged any Israelite to a one-on-one contest. Saul and his men were terrified, but God arranged for David to arrive at the battle lines at that exact time. David fought and killed Goliath and led the Israelites in a rout of the Philistine army.

7. Following the victory, the Israelite women praised David more than Saul. This was the first that Saul took special note of David. The women's praise of David galled Saul.

8. Saul took David into his army, and David was extremely successful. The more David advanced, the more Saul felt threatened.

9. Saul made attempts on David's life, first indirectly setting David up for defeat by the Philistines, then personally with a spear, next through hit men on special assignment, and finally by trying to hunt David down with the help of the Israelite army.

10. Saul's pursuit of David became an obsession that caused him to lash out at his own men and anyone else who seemed to stand in his way. Saul killed 85 priests because one of them had helped David (not knowing that David was running from Saul).

11. Saul quit chasing David when David went to live with the Philistines.

12. Two years later, the Philistine army came against Saul. Since the Lord would not speak to Saul anymore, Saul went to a witch to seek direction. The next day, he was wounded in battle and committed suicide to avoid being taken alive by the Philistines.

How anger deceived Saul.

These are the major events in which Saul's bitterness germinated and thrived. As anger developed in Saul, he did things that make us wonder, "Saul, what are you thinking?" The deceitfulness of anger is incredible.

All of Saul's distorted thoughts cannot be reconstructed. But following are some of the ways anger deceived Saul:

1. *Saul believed the praise for David was a personal slight against himself.* As already mentioned, the women of Israel were unkind to compare David and Saul publicly. But the more the Lord prospered David, the more the people sang his praises. If Saul had retained his humility and love for the Lord, he might well have loved this young man, even as Jonathan loved him. But Saul was of a different mind. His desire for the praise of men had awakened some time before when Jonathan had successfully attacked a Philistine garrison. "Let the Hebrews hear!" Saul had proclaimed. To have this upstart from Bethlehem receiving the praises of Israel grated on Saul's ego. From the first that David was so praised, the Bible records that "Saul eyed David from that day and forward" (1 Samuel 18:9). This is a jealous anger, and jealousy hears a rival's praises as a personal insult.

   The truth was that David's victories were worthy of praise. Had Saul's heart been as pure as Jonathan's, he might well have joined in thanking God for a man who could fight for Israel so effectively.

2. *Saul viewed David's accomplishments as a personal threat.* David's success shot fear through Saul's thinking. As David grew in military experience, Saul's insecurity ballooned. He saw "takeover" threats in every advancement David made against the Philistines.

It is true that God had appointed David to be the next king, but David was not organizing a plot to take over the kingdom. He made every effort to honor Saul. As time went on, David actually fled to avoid confrontation and forceful takeover. But in Saul's mind, David became an enemy, a man to be eliminated. Such is the thinking of jealous anger.

The truth was that David's victories were a blessing to Saul and to all Israel. David was a man sorely needed in Saul's army.

3. *In Saul's anger and bitterness, David's "wrongs" grew larger and larger.* Saul's fear of David taking over the kingdom seems to have turned into a feeling that David was personally doing him wrong. And the more successful David was, the more wrong he became in Saul's mind. This kind of deception thrives in a climate of jealous anger. When a person angrily views another as a rival, he will interpret the actions and words of his rival as wrongs. And they will accumulate exponentially; that is, one wrong is added to another wrong to make four wrongs, and those four wrongs are somehow squared in the mathematics of jealousy to make sixteen wrongs. There is no end to the growth of hatred.

The truth is, sometimes people do wrong us. But if we grow bitter, and particularly if we are jealous, we will find wrongs where there have been no wrongs. When imagined wrongs become part of our thinking, we have become lovers of untruth, willing to put light for darkness and darkness for light.

4. *Saul felt his personal interests were more important than the national good.* Saul would not have said this, but as he moved to push David aside, and even to take his life, this distorted thinking emerged. Saul came to the

point that he would rather have had a weaker army than have someone other than himself receiving honor.

The truth was Saul had not come to his position by his own doing, and it was not his responsibility to protect his kingship. Saul could have found much joy in putting the nation's good ahead of his personal reputation and honor.

5. *Saul believed the personal threat David was to him justified murder.* At first, Saul kept this thought well hidden. He expected David to be killed in battle with the Philistines. Instead, David grew greater. As time went on, the plots against David's life became more and more bold, until it was national news. Every open effort to harm another is preceded by secret malicious desires. As those desires take root, they distort thinking until the bitter person works openly against his rival or unashamedly plots his destruction.

The truth was that David was not a threat to Saul, but rather, an asset; and even if he had been a threat, seeking the Lord's guidance would have been the proper route for Saul, not pursuing David.

6. *Saul believed any means could be used to protect his personal interests.* Saul's attempts on David's life turned into involved plots, lies, murder of innocents, and costly army expeditions. Saul was not only murderous, but he also became domineering, vengeful, unreasonable, accusing, and deceitful. He hurled a spear at his own son, killed 85 innocent priests, sent other men to carry out his wicked plans, and wasted the time and resources of the nation's army in pursuit of David. And all this to destroy a man vitally needed by the nation! Saul, what WERE you thinking! When bitterness takes up residence in the heart, ability to discern

accurately is lost. The pathetic irony is that the smallest wrong, real or imagined, by his "enemy" may "justify" the bitter person doing far worse wrongs himself.

The truth is that God's people must not step over moral boundaries, even when the cause is right. A right end does not justify a wrong means. Anger and bitterness make people especially vulnerable to the twisted thinking that if someone else is wrong, I can use whatever means I choose to deal with that person.

7. *Saul thought he would have been all right if the circumstances would have changed.* Angry Saul saw his problems as being in his surroundings. If only David would be eliminated ... if only his men would cooperate ... if only Jonathan would not befriend David. ... Circumstances certainly can be part of a problem. That is what makes focusing on them so deceptive. Angry thinking, however, focuses solely on the outside circumstances. But unfortunately, the most frustrating circumstances are usually those we have no control over anyway. This deception leads to wasting huge amounts of mental and emotional energy, as we kick against walls that will not budge—circumstances we cannot change.

The truth was that Saul's largest problems lay in his own heart, not in his circumstances. Furthermore, when we face difficult circumstances, the effect of those circumstances on us will depend more on our attitude toward them than on the circumstances themselves. As one author stated, "Life is ten percent what happens to us and ninety percent our attitude toward what happens to us."

8. *Saul thought he could carry out his plans regardless of the Lord's purposes.* Samuel had told Saul he was rejected as

king and the Lord had appointed another man who would honor and obey Him. Eventually Saul even acknowledged David would be the next king. But Saul continued to pursue David's life in an attempt to secure his own dynasty. Bitter people operating under anger's deception disobey their parents, oppose church leaders, and even go against Bible principles in pursuit of their agenda.

The truth is that every plan or purpose of man that is against the purposes of God is doomed to fail. At times it may seem to prosper. The time came when David went to the Philistines and was out of Saul's way, but God still accomplished His purposes. Saul was rejected, and David became king. Any seeming progress against the will of God is only a delusion that precedes a terrible awakening. God will have His way.

9. *Saul believed people were against him who actually were for him.* We have already noted how this was so with David, but it was true with others also. Saul accused Jonathan of plotting against him; he accused his soldiers of being secretly aligned with David; he accused the priests of forming a conspiracy with David against him. Anger poisoned his thinking, making him suspicious and resentful, causing him to lash out at people who were actually helping him. Bitterness can become so ingrained that even loving actions of Christian friends may trigger angry, resentful responses from the bitter person.

The truth was that David, Jonathan, Saul's men, and the priests were loyal to Saul and the nation of Israel. Bitterness blinds. It robs the bitter person of the ability to discern between friends and enemies, between good and evil designs.

10. *Saul believed he was a victim.* When he accused his men of conspiracy with David, he pouted, "There is none of you that is sorry for me" (1 Samuel 22:8). Victim thinking grows naturally out of blame thinking. It holds others responsible for things they have not done, and makes us blind to our own responsibility for our actions. Victim thinking drips with self-pity. It crafts subtle ways to make others feel guilty. It projects helplessness on the surface, but underneath it is a means of controlling others. By putting up a sorry front, the "victim" is manipulating others to conform to his will. At the same time, he is setting up barriers against anyone approaching him with his responsibility—by shedding tears, he safeguards himself against others doing anything to upset him further.

The truth was that Saul was not a victim. He was victimizing others. Saul did not need pity; he needed to repent of his disobedience, jealousy, and anger. Saul was not helpless in his problems; he could have turned to the Lord and found mercy and grace. On the other hand, some people are victims of other persons' evil doings. When the victim mentality sets in, however, it will cause us to develop a pattern of crying, "I'm a victim! It's not my fault!" when in truth we are responsible. It is furthermore true, as we will explore later, that in Christ we can be more than conquerors, even when we are the victims of the worst of atrocities.

11. *Saul believed nobody understood his situation.* We see this reflected at various times in his verbal tirades. It is a common deception of those who grow bitter. The more distorted their thinking becomes, the harder they try to get people to see things their way. And the harder they try, the more impatient and less

understanding others are likely to become. What bitter people usually want is for someone to agree with their way of seeing a situation, justifying themselves, and blaming others. The more their minds churn in the muddy waters of bitterness, the more "evidence" they will find against others and for their own position. But the muddier the evidence, the less inclined people are to believe them.

Bitter people walk around, as it were, with a sack over their shoulders, carrying all the wrongs others have done to them. They have a variety of ways of arousing others' curiosity about what is in the sack, such as walking doubled over under the weight of these problems or hinting about the terrible things stored in their sack. They can bring their problems into conversations on nearly any topic. When they get a listening ear, they take down their sack and begin pulling out juicy spoilage from their past. When a discerning friend questions their bent reasoning, they respond with something like, "Oh, I haven't told you the half!" And into the sack they go for more. If an honest and committed friend suggests the bitter person must leave his bitterness, the bitter person will typically respond, "You just don't understand." At that point, he usually throws his sack over his shoulder and walks off in a huff to find someone else who will listen.

The truth is, there are usually people in the bitter person's life who understand him better than he is willing to acknowledge. More basically, the problem is not people misunderstanding the bitter person's situation, but they are uncomfortable and unsympathetic with the bitter person's underlying motives.

12. *Saul thought being a victim obligated others to help him get his*

way. The mentality of a victim is self-centered. Saul's world revolved around himself, and the more it did, the worse his problems grew. People's lack of cooperation fuels a victim's thinking that he is being wronged, which in turn makes him believe even more strongly that others are obligated to help him. When the bitter person is in power, this vicious cycle becomes especially nasty. Saul's men were willing to go after David, and they took Saul's scoldings stoically, but when commanded to kill the priests, they were trapped. On the one hand was a deranged king's order, and on the other, the realization these were holy men who did not deserve to die.

The truth is that no amount of victimization justifies unrighteous responses or obligates others to cooperate with unrighteous responses. It is right to stand with, understand, and give loving support to true victims. But Saul was not a victim. No one is obligated to cooperate with plans motivated by jealousy, hatred, or ill will.

13. *Saul believed if people did not agree with him, they were against him.* Saul wanted people on his side. He thought in terms of his world and his causes alone. Uncooperative people landed on his black list and were in danger of wrath, accusation, and harm. In 1 Chronicles 12, we find a long list of defectors from Saul's army, "even of Saul's brethren of Benjamin" (v. 2). These were men who fell out of favor with Saul, for whatever reason, and "fell to [David] . . . day by day . . . until it was a great host, like the host of God" (vv. 20, 22). Some of these men demonstrated outstanding loyalty in service to David. Saul simply had no time or use for people not totally agreed with him nor operating by his agenda. By forcing people to

line up with his cause, he pushed his best people away.

The truth is good people do disagree with plans born of wrong motives. Their disagreement does not mean they are disloyal; loyalty may in fact motivate them to disagree. Good people realize the real dividing line is not between being for or against a bitter person, but between being for or against God. No man or woman is big enough to demand other people to be either for or against them. Only Jesus is a person significant enough, only God's cause of eternal salvation through His Son is a cause significant enough to say, "He that is not for us is against us." When bitter people, like Saul, try to force others to be either totally for them or against them, they are deluded.

14. *Saul believed others had motives similar to his own.* Saul became mean and vindictive. The more evil motives drove Saul's mind and behavior, the more suspicious he grew of others. He secretly plotted against David and assumed David was plotting against him. He hid his true motives from his men and assumed his men were secretly working against him. Behind a good face, he assigned secret missions and schemed evil, and he assumed the priests had evil plans hidden behind their righteous service. Such is the deception of bitterness. It becomes so familiar with treachery that it cannot trust, so acquainted with malice that it cannot believe people would love purely, so adept at wearing masks that it suspects every honest man's face, so steeped in selfishness that it cannot believe others are capable of sacrificial loyalty. The evil motivations that churn in the bitter person's heart are subconsciously transferred to others.

The truth was Saul doubted and accused men who

were trustworthy and blameless. Evil motives destroy the ability to discern the true motives of others.

15. *By blaming others, Saul became blind to how he could have corrected his own sins.* This deception led to the tragedy of Saul's death. He spent his life pursuing revenge instead of repentance. We could well wonder how the Biblical record might have been different if Saul had laid down his grudge against David and had sought the Lord. Saul may not have changed God's purposes for transferring the kingdom to David, but he could have changed his attitude and position in relation to God's purposes. By focusing on what he wanted, however, and by keeping his finger pointed at others, Saul could not see the steps to repentance. He was blind to how he could have brought unity to the nation and peace to his own heart. "He that loveth his brother abideth in the light, and there is none occasion of stumbling in him. But he that hateth his brother is in darkness, and walketh in darkness, and knoweth not whither he goeth, because that darkness hath blinded his eyes" (1 John 2:10, 11).

The truth is that no person can keep us from repentance and finding God's blessing in our own lives. The barrier to joy in Saul's life was the wickedness in his own heart.

16. *Saul doubted God's goodness and denied God's interest in him personally.* Observing the dismal emotional and spiritual condition in which Saul sought direction from a witch, we could weep. "I am sore distressed; for the Philistines make war against me, and God is departed from me, and answereth me no more, neither by prophets, nor by dreams: therefore I have called thee, that thou mayest make known unto me what I shall do" (1 Samuel 28:15).

The truth is that "the LORD is nigh unto them that are of a broken heart; and saveth such as be of a contrite spirit" (Psalm 34:18). David, the man Saul despised, wrote those words; but Saul, absorbed as he was in his anger and bitterness, was blind to the goodness of God.

There were surely more than 16 deceptions that affected Saul's thinking, but these are enough to demonstrate that anger and bitterness distort perspective. The person who holds to his anger enters a darkness, and in that darkness he judges people and interprets events through twisted logic and carnal motivations.

All these deceptions, however, have to do with what was going on inside of Saul himself. Bitterness is not only a personal problem, but also an interpersonal one.

How bitterness is deceptive in interpersonal relationships.

Many of the interpersonal evidences of bitterness are overt and obvious. A bitter person, for example, develops patterns of blaming others, complaining, pitying himself, and has problems living under authority. These evidences are not hard to discern. Although the bitter person may be deceived and may vehemently deny bitterness, those around him can easily see bitterness is the root problem.

Other symptoms of bitterness are less obvious. Bitterness is like a root growing underground; the place it "springs up" may be so far removed from the area of bitterness that there would seem to be no connection. If we get beneath the surface, however, we can see the problem is directly tied to bitterness in the heart. Let's consider several examples:

1. *Intemperate pursuits.* Steve was a 16-year-old boy who lived and breathed softball. He would rather have played softball with his youth group than anything

else. He let nothing stand in the way of his playing, including a health problem and his parents' concern about how hard and how often he played. Steve's father believed softball was foolishness. If he had had his way, Steve would not have played at all, certainly not regularly. Beneath the tension about softball was a broken father-son relationship that went back for years. Steve's father had always made work his priority. Family fun, the children's interests, and home activities were often sacrificed for work.

Numerous other factors contributed to Steve's troubles with his father, but the bottom line was that Steve was bitterly angry. He felt unloved, inferior, and cheated. If anyone would have asked Steve if he pursued softball with such fervor because he was bitter toward his dad, he would have scoffed at the idea. But many times the fuel behind an intemperate pursuit is unresolved bitterness. The more a parent opposes the pursuit of a bitter son or daughter, the more they are driven to pursue it.

Bitter people have a way of finding each other. A young man like Steve will easily be drawn to a young woman with similar problems and attitudes. On the surface their relationship seems to be one of understanding and sensitivity. They feel like balm for each other. And the more their parents object, the more balm they will need and willingly give.

Nobody can convince them they are not good for each other. If anyone would suggest they are more motivated by bitterness than by love, they would think that person to be totally wrong. But again, when a bitter person ardently pursues something, more often than not, the force driving that pursuit is the fire of bitterness burning within. After Mr. and Mrs.

Bitter get married, reality sets in. They find the balm they were using was acidic. They were only spreading the infection, not treating it. They soon find that bitterness in the intimate relationship of marriage is more hurtful than it was in their former relationship with their parents. The injuries only multiply. The pain only increases.

2. *Know-it-all attitude.* This covert symptom of bitterness grows out of the inner devastation surrounding bitterness. Often, bitter people have been deeply hurt—rejected, abused, neglected, etc. Sometimes, as in Saul's case, the bitterness rises out of some form of self-centered anger, such as jealousy. But in any case, the bitter person feels like a "zero person," a nobody. When this inferiority has been fed by regular attacks against one's person—name calling, criticism, sarcasm—the buildup of inner frustration is sometimes vented in grandiose talk. Without understanding himself, he is trying to cover who he fears he is— a nobody, a simpleton, an incompetent. The person absorbs information, diagnoses problems, and prescribes solutions, all in an effort to project an image of competence.

When bitterness drives a person to establish his identity, relationships suffer. What the bitter person desperately wants is acceptance, but his arrogance only estranges him further. He makes claims that are hard to believe. He often challenges established procedures. He delights in showing up the errors of experts. He farms differently, builds differently, drives differently, schedules differently, manages differently, and doctors differently just to prove that he knows best.

But behind the mask, under the confident front, is a

lonely person. Others can't get close to him, and he knows it and feels it. His loneliness only adds to his drive to be somebody significant. The know-it-all will sometimes let people get close to him to a certain extent when he is in trouble, as he often is. But once he is on his feet again, his besetting sin easily takes over and he is off again thinking big thoughts, making big plans, erecting the big facade that says, "I'm somebody!"

3. *Control tactics.* Not all people who try to control others are bitter, but all who are bitter try to control. Sometimes a bitter person's control tactics are overt (as for example, in an outburst of anger—controlling by making others back off), but many times the control tactics are subtle and have no seeming connection to bitterness. Some methods of control, in fact, seem pleasant on the surface.

To understand why a bitter person tries to control others, we need to understand that a bitter person is fighting an emotional warfare against situations or people he cannot change. He may go over and over events that have happened in the past and can never be undone, or he may spend his free time mentally arguing with or outmaneuvering a person he resents. In any case, the bitter person is struggling against what is beyond his control. But the tendency is to think of ways to bring the situation and people back under control.

Some people, like King Saul, are in a position to control. Others, without authority, learn more subtle ways of managing situations and people. Following are a few examples of control tactics subtle enough that, on the surface, they do not seem related to bitterness:

a. *Flattery: saying nice things about (or doing favors for) people in order to obligate them to be nice in return or to side with the bitter person.* A bitter person can be extremely kind, courteous, and even sacrificial if it is to his advantage. Although the bitter person would deny it, his flattery or favor is almost invariably an attempt to prove something to the one(s) he is bitter toward.

b. *Being confidential: sharing private information to secure people's friendship and obligate their trust, especially if the bitter person does not want these people to get closer to the one he is bitter toward.* The writer of the proverbs wisely said, "Make no friendship with an angry man" (Proverbs 22:24). The motives of a bitter person are so hidden that even he would seldom understand he is being confidential and friendly more because of ill will toward others than goodwill toward his "friend."

c. *Giving veiled signals of needs: hinting in roundabout ways that something is wrong, but not being specific or open.* This is often a subconscious way of controlling caring people—manipulating them to give their kind attention. Following is a typical conversation showing how a bitter person tries to control a caring person:

> Caring Connie: "Hi, Betty. How are you doing?"
> Bitter Betty: "Oh, I'll be all right."
> Caring Connie: "Is something wrong?"
> Bitter Betty: "Oh, it's nothing. I'll be okay."
> Caring Connie: "Are you sure?"
> Bitter Betty: "It's just more of the same."
> Caring Connie: "Are you having problems with your mom again?"
> Bitter Betty: "Just the normal."

Caring Connie: "Do you want to talk about it?"
Bitter Betty: "I don't see what good it would do."

This conversation typically drags on until Connie has pulled the whole story out of Betty. Notice Betty pretended it was a small thing and not necessary to talk about (and probably it wasn't). But if Connie had not taken the time to draw it out of her, Betty would have been deeply hurt. Betty tries to control people like Connie as a direct result of bitterness.

The above examples of control tactics are only samples. A bitter person can turn virtually every contact with others into an opportunity to control. The real problem is not his control tactics, but the bitterness that drives him to control people.

Veiled control tactics, like intemperate pursuits and a know-it-all attitude, are covert symptoms of bitterness. On the surface we may not see the connection between these interpersonal problems and bitterness, but this only emphasizes how deceptive bitterness really is.

People who are driven and people who are know-it-alls and people who try to control others create conflict. Unfortunately, it is far easier to focus on the surface symptoms than on the root problem. The father focuses on the son's disobedience and intemperance. People criticize the know-it-all or argue with him or turn away in disgust. The controlling person is avoided as much as possible. But until the root of bitterness is dealt with, there is no lasting remedy for the surface problems.

The deception of bitterness could well bring us to despair. With the Apostle Paul, we might cry, "Who can deliver us from this wretched condition?" Paul found deliverance from sin's power to be in Jesus Christ. Through Christ there is deliverance for every sin. In the following chapters we will look at remedies for anger and bitterness.

Study Questions (Chapter Three)

1. To better understand the change that occurred in Saul, read each of the following verses in its context and describe the character quality you see in Saul.
   a. 1 Samuel 9:5
   b. 1 Samuel 9:21
   c. 1 Samuel 10:16
   d. 1 Samuel 10:22
   e. 1 Samuel 10:27
   f. 1 Samuel 11:6
   g. 1 Samuel 11:13

2. The exact turning point in Saul's life is not clear. Perhaps there were several turning points. What do you see as significant about Saul's character in each of the following verses?
   a. 1 Samuel 13:3
   b. 1 Samuel 13:8-12
   c. 1 Samuel 14:24
   d. 1 Samuel 15:9
   e. 1 Samuel 15:30

3. What did Saul fear in David?

4. How did Saul's fear feed his anger?

5. List a number of things Saul accused David of.

6. Do you think Saul actually believed these things, or did he use them as excuses to pursue David?

7. List the attempts Saul made on David's life. Roughly estimate the cost of Saul's efforts.

8. List the people in Saul's life whom he turned against.

9. How did Saul emotionally manipulate his men (1 Samuel 22)?

10. Scan through 1 Chronicles 12 and list the groups of people who defected to David.

11. What do these defections indicate about Saul's character?

12. Describe the thinking of a victim.

13. Describe how anger distorts our thinking about other people beyond the one we are angry toward.

14. Describe how anger distorts our thinking about God.

15. What is the danger of two bitter people getting married?

16. Bitter people typically become controllers. Study Acts 8:13-24 for an example of a bitter man obsessed with power. What control tactics do you see in Simon?

17. What is the deceptive thinking behind the control tactics of a bitter person?

PART 2

PUTTING AWAY ANGER AND BITTERNESS

CHAPTER 4

EMOTION-BASED RESPONSES VERSUS BIBLE-BASED RESPONSES

"You know, I thank God for my depression." Sandra's eyes misted even as she spoke. "I believe He is using this experience to accomplish things in my life I don't fully understand at this point."

Five months earlier, Sandra had felt rejected at home. Though an excellent teacher, she had felt rejected by the school board, by her fellow teachers, by her students, and by their parents. Sandra had developed emotion-based response patterns that spiraled deeper and deeper into depression. When her psychiatrist lightly brushed off her feelings, Sandra had angrily taken a lethal overdose of pills.

Learning new responses to difficulties did not come easily for Sandra, but over time she found answers. People bound by anger and bitterness can find freedom. An important step is understanding the difference between emotion-based responses and Bible-based responses.

Understanding Emotion-Based Responses

In Chapter 1, we learned emotions act as reflectors. Our internal feelings reflect what is going on around us. We also noted that the kind of emotional reflections we have in any situation depends on the kind of person we are. We are constantly responding emotionally to our circumstances. Let's explore this further.

1. *Everyone faces situations that stir deep feelings.* Some situations are more painful than others, and yet no one's life is free from deep feelings of pain, frustration, or grief. It is not wrong to feel deeply. Many of the psalms are expressions of the writer's deep feelings, feelings that rose out of terrible situations.

2. *Some difficult situations are ongoing.* David was hounded by Saul for years. Abigail lived with a husband so quarrelsome that his servants avoided speaking to him if possible. Life seemed to dish out one injustice after another to Joseph. It is one thing to go through a difficult experience. It is definitely worse when the difficulty doesn't go away and there is no end in sight. In ongoing suffering, deep feelings of frustration, confusion, and anguish multiply.

3. *Deep feelings press for verbal and behavioral responses.* Feelings are powerful motivators of behavior. They call for words. They demand action. They urge us to change the situation, correct it, punish the offenders, and set things straight. But usually there are forces at work beyond our control. We have little power to change wrong behavior in people around us. We cannot control storms that destroy property. We have no authority over disease and death. The knowledge that we are helpless to change a situation may deepen our frustration into rage; and the stronger the feelings within us, the more urgently they call for action.

4. *Responses based on feelings develop into patterns.* When a person is angry, he will be urged to act in a certain way. What he does and says, based on anger, will

easily be repeated the next time he feels angry. With repeated provocations to anger, he will likely develop habitual responses. Consider the following illustrations of emotion-based response patterns:

- Perry has another argument with his dad; he squeals his tires going out the driveway.

- Starla's husband is late for supper the third night in a row; she is silently angry all evening, giving only monosyllable responses to her husband and children.

- Lisa gets a poor grade on a test; when she comes home, she goes straight to her room, slams the door, and shuts herself in for the rest of the evening.

- George's wife does not comply with his standards for her appearance; he heatedly calls her liberal and unsubmissive, and she lashes back that he is ultra-conservative and a dictator.

- Jane feels people are always slighting her; inwardly she reviews her hurts in detail again and again. She talks and looks wretched most of the time.

- Carla was sexually abused as a child; she regularly challenges men, points out where they are wrong, and projects an image of competence. But underneath she is hurting and angry.

- Wade was regularly put down in his home and among his peers while growing up; today he is demanding of his wife and children. They can do nothing quickly enough or well enough to avoid his criticism.

These individuals have developed predictable response patterns based on deep feelings. They have developed their emotion-based response patterns over a period of time as they faced trying situations.

The patterns demonstrated on the previous page could be listed in various ways, but notice the following categories of emotion-based patterns:

a. *Temper patterns: an explosive outburst or an inward seething against something or someone who displeases me.* When expressed outwardly, words are harsh, loud, and accusing; actions are rash and destructive. If held inside, it is no less a temper pattern than an outburst. The major difference is that the explosive temper damages everyone nearby; whereas, the person who internalizes his anger primarily harms himself.

b. *Blame patterns: focusing on all the ways others are responsible for my problems.* Words are critical and loaded with accusations and insinuations; actions revolve around the desire to exact a price. Blame patterns are accompanied by defensiveness and a super-sensitivity to what others are saying or doing in relation to the bitter person.

c. *Victim patterns: finding security in not being responsible.* Words drip with self-pity, sadness, and complaint; actions are often restrained, even lethargic. The victim is constantly on the lookout for hurts and slights.

d. *Control patterns: manipulating or pressuring people by causing emotional misery until they do what I want.* Words, actions, and attitudes are combined in countless ways to make others feel guilty or afraid or miserable, pushing or pulling them into place.

Angry, bitter people are ALWAYS controllers in some way.

Let's return to understanding more about emotion-based responses.

5. *Emotion-based responses are natural.* We do not need to develop a pattern of behaving and speaking based on how we feel; it comes naturally. Because it is natural, it feels right. And because it becomes habitual, we are hardly aware of how we are responding. Others, however, are keenly aware of our emotion-based patterns and generally resent them.

6. *When our behavior and words are based on our emotions, we will do and say things that add to our problems.* Looking back over the examples of emotion-based responses, we can easily see they do not make for good relationships. Each person's response is now making things worse for himself and for others. In fact, each is no doubt stirring deep feelings in other people, feelings that have the potential of developing into similar emotion-based responses in them.

7. *Patterns of emotion-based responses lead to bondage.* Habits in word and action based on emotions such as anger, frustration, and resentment become more and more ingrained as the months and years go by. As they progress, so do their consequences. Emotion-based responses bog people deeper and deeper into the mire of carnality. Frustration becomes a prison. Self-pity shackles its victims. Resentment, ill will, pouting, a critical spirit, and jealousy forge chains around the mind and will until the person cannot break out of his patterns even when he wants to.

Sometimes in the misery accompanying these emotion-based response patterns, people do want to change. They come to see themselves for what they are—angry, depressed, and miserable. They suddenly see they have been pouting, accusing, controlling others, and pitying themselves; and they resolve to change . . . only to find themselves two days later as deeply mired in their patterns as ever.

There is hope! Some people attempt to change through education and discipline. Those efforts are not all bad, but spiritual bondage demands spiritual deliverance. Jesus Christ is the Deliverer. No bondage is too difficult for Him. Every fetter of sin and Satan must yield when Jesus takes charge of one's life.

Understanding Bible-Based Responses

When we face difficult situations, it is natural to respond to our feelings. It is not wrong to feel deep emotions when we face difficulty, but it is dangerous to base our responses on these feelings. Our feelings will drag us into the mire of carnality.

How then should we respond? Bible-based responses often stand in contrast to emotion-based responses as we will see in the following points:

1. *Bible-based responses come to us from God's Word.* God is vitally concerned about how we speak and act in difficult situations—situations that would naturally make us angry, resentful, or bitter. God's Word provides us with alternatives to our natural responses. In the midst of trial, injustice, and pain, how we feel is not the only consideration. Let's be balanced in acknowledging that God cares about how we feel. He is not insensitive to our frustration, confusion, grief, or pain. But we need far more than our feelings as a base for discerning how we should respond under such conditions. We need the

sure Word of God. We need direction that does not change with circumstances, guidance that does not go up and down with our emotions. We need wisdom beyond our limited understanding. The Word of God is rock-sure, and it does give practical guidance for God's children when they are in the fires of difficulty.

2. *Bible-based responses often go against our natural sensibilities.* Following God's directions in trying circumstances does not always make sense to us—specifically, it does not make sense to the natural man. For "the natural man receiveth not the things of the Spirit of God: for they are foolishness unto him: neither can he know them, because they are spiritually discerned" (1 Corinthians 2:14). Furthermore, following God's directions may mean doing exactly the opposite of what we feel like doing. We follow God's directions, then, not because we feel like it, but because God's directions are right.

3. *Bible-based responses do not ignore reality.* The Bible is not naive or flippant. It does not require that we deny our pain, nor does it excuse the wrongs and sins of those around us as "all right." We will look at this further in the next chapter. For now let's be clear that Bible-based responses allow us to face our situation honestly, but in the context of the larger truth of God. When we view difficulty apart from an awareness of God, we get one picture; when we include God, His wisdom, His higher purposes, and His grace, we see the same situation, but in a light that completely changes the perspective.

4. *Bible-based responses develop into patterns.* Just as we noted earlier that carnality becomes habitual when we base our responses on feelings like anger, resentment, or self-pity, so it is with Bible-based responses.

The more we exercise ourselves in God's ways, the more they become our pattern of behavior. Even as people come to expect a pouter to pout when things don't go as expected, so people come to expect a believer to look to God when faced with the same disappointment. Bible-based responses become a way of life.

Just what kinds of patterns develop when we base our responses on God's Word instead of on our feelings? Following are several examples:

a. *Faith patterns: believing that God is in total charge of my life and that He will allow nothing in my experience that will frustrate His good purposes for me.* "Trust in the LORD with all thine heart; and lean not unto thine own understanding. In all thy ways acknowledge him, and he shall direct thy paths" (Proverbs 3:5, 6).

b. *Forgiveness patterns: releasing those who do wrong to me on a personal level and laying down the demand for a "price" for their wrong.* "Forgive us our debts, as we forgive our debtors. For if ye forgive men their trespasses, your heavenly Father will also forgive you: But if ye forgive not men their trespasses, neither will your Father forgive your trespasses" (Matthew 6:12, 14, 15).

c. *Love patterns: speaking and acting toward people in ways that convey kindness, goodwill, and compassion; being committed to the highest good of others even at personal cost.* "By this shall all men know that ye are my disciples, if ye have love one to another" (John 13:35). "Love your enemies, bless them that curse you, do good to them that hate you, and pray for them which despitefully use you, and persecute you" (Matthew 5:44).

    d. *Gratitude patterns: expressing appreciation to God and others for how they have contributed to my life.* "In every thing give thanks: for this is the will of God in Christ Jesus concerning you" (1 Thessalonians 5:18).

    e. *Intercession patterns: bringing the needs of others to the Father, making request for them as if the needs were my own.* "I exhort therefore, that, first of all, supplications, prayers, intercessions, and giving of thanks, be made for all men" (1 Timothy 2:1). "Praying always with all prayer and supplication in the Spirit, and watching thereunto with all perseverance and supplication for all saints" (Ephesians 6:18).

We could continue with examples of Bible-based patterns, but to see them even more clearly, contrast them with the emotion-based patterns discussed earlier. Note that each of the preceding examples is based on clear direction from God's Word and that the direction is specifically for God's children when facing unpleasant situations—situations that would naturally make us feel angry, frustrated, bitter, etc.

Let's return, now, to a few more points about faith-based responses.

5. *Patterns of Bible-based responses are liberating.* Emotion-based patterns result in bondage—patterns of resentment, for example, bind up the heart in blame and self-pity and shackle the mind to perform endless routines in misery. Bible-based patterns, in contrast, free the soul. The heart is set free to praise and worship the Creator and Sustainer of life. The mind is free to be creative and purposeful in following the will of God. "I will RUN the way of thy commandments" the psalmist exults (Psalm 119:32).

6. *Bible-based patterns result in an entirely different emotional atmosphere.* The natural feelings we have in times of difficulty are unsafe grounds for action. They lead into more and more misery. When, in spite of those feelings, we choose to respond according to God's directions, a surprising change results in our feelings. We have the rich awareness of the Lord's presence, the joy of His blessing on our responses, the wonder of His grace and goodness, the pleasant surprise of insights into God's higher ways, and the satisfaction of knowing we are doing right.

7. *Bible-based responses release God's power in our behalf.* "For the eyes of the LORD run to and fro throughout the whole earth, to shew himself strong in the behalf of them whose heart is perfect toward him [that is, completely devoted to Him]" (2 Chronicles 16:9). When God's people trust in Him, He works powerfully in their behalf. This is in contrast to when we follow our own inclinations, based on our natural feelings. At such times, we only make matters worse. Bible-based responses honor the Lord, and thus they have His blessing.

Many people are hurting. Unfortunately, by following their natural feelings in response to their hurts, they only add to their problems. Hurting people easily develop patterns of responses that hurt others. The vicious cycle of sin, carnality, and pain is broken only when people turn in faith from their own ways to the Lord. As they learn to base their responses on God's Word, they receive grace not only to break the bonds of anger and bitterness in their own lives, but also to become agents of healing and help in the lives of others.

Study Questions (Chapter Four)

1. In 1 Samuel 25 we have an account in which people felt strong emotions and acted on them. Look at each of the following verses and describe how the person felt, and how that feeling affected his or her response:
   a. Nabal, vv. 10, 11
   b. David, vv. 13, 21
   c. Abigail, v. 18
   d. Nabal, v. 36

2. Read Abigail's logic in vv. 30, 31. She understood that responses based on anger actually add to the problem. What would have happened if Abigail had not intervened?

3. What emotion-based pattern do we see operating in Nabal (v. 17)?

4. Looking at Simon (Acts 8), how do we know that bitterness had progressed to a form of bondage?

5. What signs betray bondage to anger or bitterness?

6. What particular form of anger or expression of anger do you struggle with?

7. Bible-based responses often go contrary to how we feel. In each of the following verses tell how we would naturally feel, and then tell how the Bible directs us:
   a. Matthew 5:11, 12
   b. Matthew 5:44
   c. James 1:2
   d. James 1:9

8. In each of the following Scriptures, tell what the natural feeling would have been, and then tell how the person(s) responded according to the teaching of Jesus.
   a. Acts 4:21-24
   b. Acts 5:40, 41
   c. Acts 7:59, 60
   d. Acts 13:50-52
   e. Acts 16:19-25

9. List the Bible-based response patterns given in this chapter and find additional verses that give similar direction.

10. Now find a Biblical example for each of these responses.

11. Describe some of the feelings that may follow obedience to Bible-based responses. (You may consider some of the Biblical examples above.)

12. Name and describe several emotion-based responses you have struggled with.

13. Which of the Bible-based responses do you find particularly difficult, or which do you personally need to cultivate?

14. When we honor God's ways, He honors us. Give examples from the Bible or from your experience illustrating how obedience to God resulted in a remarkable work of God.

CHAPTER 5

THE RESPONSE OF FAITH

Following our natural feelings during difficulty, we end up in emotional prisons. We are angry, resentful, bitter, self-pitying, or depressed, as the case may be. In those emotional prisons, we are cut off from the light and truth of God; and for that reason, Satan loves to have us there. "The god of this world hath blinded the minds of them which believe not, lest the light of the glorious gospel of Christ, who is the image of God, should shine unto them" (2 Corinthians 4:4).

While this verse describes Satan's work specifically in unbelievers, his tactics are identical for believers. He would like nothing better than to blind Christians to the light of God. Hebrews gives this specific warning, "Take heed, brethren, lest there be in any of you an evil heart of unbelief, in departing from the living God" (Hebrews 3:12). Faith opens our eyes to the unseeable realm; unbelief shuts our eyes to that realm. Nowhere does unbelief thrive so well as in the gloom of angry, bitter thoughts and feelings.

Christians do not deny God outright. But unfortunately, many Christians succumb to the blindness of unbelief in more subtle forms. In their anger, they may become oblivious to the power of God. They may misunderstand His purposes, even speaking bitterly against what God has allowed. They may come to doubt and deny God's goodness, His interest in them, and His promised care. If ever Christians need faith, and if ever they need the warning against unbelief, it is in those circumstances when naturally they feel angry and resentful.

What is faith?

"Now faith is the substance of things hoped for, the evidence of things not seen" (Hebrews 11:1). Or as the New American Standard Bible puts it, "Faith is the assurance of things hoped for, the conviction of things not seen."

Faith, then, is the certainty (assurance or conviction) about a reality we cannot see.

We live in a realm of time and sense. We can confirm the certainty of things in this realm through our natural senses—touch, taste, hearing, seeing, and smelling. If someone tells us, "There is a rock in your front yard," we can go to the front yard and confirm not only that it is there, but its size, color, shape, and composition.

There is another realm, however, referred to in the Bible as spiritual. This realm is not perceived through our natural senses. God is at the center of this realm, but it includes angels and evil spirits, heaven and hell, along with all the spiritual laws and principles that operate in that realm. The Bible speaks, for example, of the "law of sin and death" and the "law of the Spirit of life in Christ Jesus" (Romans 8:2). While these spiritual laws cannot be studied or demonstrated in the concrete sense that the laws of the natural realm can be (such as the law of gravity), they are nonetheless real.

The spiritual realm is distinct from the natural realm in its characteristics, but the two realms are inseparably interrelated. God, at the center of the spiritual realm, made the natural realm. And He governs it. Furthermore, there is spiritual warfare going on all the time, affecting the actions, decisions, and plans of everyday life on earth. The devil and his angels are bent on deception, destruction, and death. God is redeeming a host for His glory, and offering grace for daily living to those who follow Him.

Many people are blind to the spiritual realm. Some are vaguely aware of it. Some dabble in forbidden spiritual territory and powers. And there are others who by faith believe the revelation of God about this spiritual realm.

Because the unseen realm cannot be verified by our natural senses, we have trouble with faith. But this unseen realm is just as real as the natural world. Faith is the certainty or conviction believers have about this unseen realm.

How is faith an alternative to anger?

In situations where our natural response would be anger, God calls us to believe in Him, trust Him, and rest our lives in His care and purposes. In situations that stir our anger, certain truths become extremely important.

1. *God is.* "But without faith it is impossible to please him: for he that cometh to God must believe that he is, and that he is a rewarder of them that diligently seek him" (Hebrews 11:6). As noted in the introduction to this chapter, most Christians will not deny God outright, even when they are angry. But in times of distress, they may lose sight of Him, or they may develop distorted thoughts about Him.

   Neither faith nor unbelief establish reality. If a rock sits in my front yard, whether I believe or disbelieve it is there does not change its existence. I may shut my front curtains, declare it is not there, even write a thesis about its nonexistence; but my unbelief does not change the reality of that rock. Even so, the reality of the spiritual realm is not established by faith nor disestablished by unbelief. God is, whether I believe in Him or not.

2. *God is sovereign.* "Our God is in the heavens: he hath done whatsoever he hath pleased" (Psalm 115:3). "Whatsoever the LORD pleased, that did he in heaven, and in earth, in the seas, and all deep places" (Psalm 135:6). "And all the inhabitants of the earth are reputed as nothing: and he doeth according to his will in the army of heaven, and among the inhabitants of the earth: and none can stay his hand, or say unto him, What doest thou?" (Daniel 4:35).

These verses clearly establish the sovereignty of God over the affairs of men. How do we understand such sovereignty in light of wickedness on the earth? If God is sovereign, why is there evil? How can people choose to live contrary to His will? Theologians have long struggled to try to reconcile the sovereignty of God with man's free will. Consider the following truths:

a. *God can and does allow people to make personal choices.*

b. *God can and does place limitations on humans.* Power of choice, in other words, is limited by power of accomplishment—no amount of free will gives man the power to visit other galaxies or annul the law of gravity.

c. *God can and does hold men and women accountable for their choices.*

d. *God can and does establish consequences and rewards for man's choices.* This is so in this life and is absolute in eternity. Men and women can make choices in this life, but ultimately God alone will decide their destiny. (In Scriptural language, He already has, based on His foreknowledge, predestinated those in Christ to be with Him in eternal paradise and those outside of Christ to be severed from Him in eternal damnation.)

Let's carry forward the truths about God that can save us from the bondage of anger and bitterness.

3. *God has eternal purposes for His people.* "For I know the thoughts that I think toward you, saith the LORD, thoughts of peace, and not of evil, to give you an expected end" (Jeremiah 29:11). This promise is in the context of God's prophecies to the Jewish people. He predicted that after 70 years of captivity in Babylon, they would be restored to the land of Palestine, and they would find Him.

We may make application from this to God's people today. God has plans for every one of His children. His plans are good. And His plans always extend beyond what we are able to see at any given time. As He puts it, "For as the heavens are higher than the earth, so are my ways higher than your ways, and my thoughts than your thoughts" (Isaiah 55:9).

4. *God is able to use the very circumstances we are facing to accomplish His good purposes in our lives.* "And we know that all things work together for good to them that love God, to them who are the called according to his purpose" (Romans 8:28).

This verse assures us of the sovereignty of God over a sinful world. People can and do violate the will of God. They sin against His express commandments. They also sin against other people. But neither the sinner nor the situation he creates ever gets out from under the sovereign hand of God. In the lives of those who love God and trust in Him, God is at work in all situations to bring about His good purposes in spite of the choices others are making.

This sovereignty defies full understanding by any human being, much less a full explanation. We do not need to understand how God works all things together for our good. We need only to trust that He is able to do so.

5. *God's purposes for us include bringing out of our lives a message of His power and grace.* Paul told the Corinthian Christians their lives were like a letter "known and read of all men" (2 Corinthians 3:2). He told the young believers at Thessalonica that although they had "received the word in much affliction," their testimony was going out so powerfully "that we need not to speak any thing" (1 Thessalonians 1:6, 8).

When people place their faith in God, He is able to turn their problems into life messages that testify of Him. Those looking on do not so much think about the difficulties as they think about the Deliverer. The Bible is filled with such examples, confirming the words of a prophet (actually given in rebuke to a man who didn't trust God). "The eyes of the LORD run to and fro throughout the whole earth, to shew himself strong in the behalf of them whose heart is perfect [fully devoted] toward him" (2 Chronicles 16:9).

6. *God's purposes for us are higher than we can see.* When God took the Israelites out of Egypt, He had much more in mind than simply getting them out of a difficult situation. When He predicted Joseph would rule over his brothers, He had much more in mind than simply giving Joseph a position. As a young man facing the

test of forbidden meat, did Daniel know all God had in mind for him in Babylon? When Paul and Silas were beaten and thrown into jail, did they know about the coming earthquake and the jailer's conversion?

The answer to these questions is obvious. The sobering truth is that the mighty and far-reaching effects of these situations came about as God's children placed their faith in Him. And we may well wonder on the other hand how many good purposes of God have gone unfulfilled due to unbelief. The eyes of the Lord truly are searching the earth for those who will exercise faith in Him in times of difficulty.

These are hard truths for us actually to live by. To the natural man, they are foolishness. But to the person willing to live by faith, these truths are life-giving and liberating. On the basis of the above truths, though our situation may be out of our control, it is not out of God's control. Though presently miserable, its long-term effect on our life will be good.

Every child of God faces situations that test his faith, situations that seem to disprove the truths we just noted from the Word of God. Sometimes we face situations in which it seems God ISN'T—or at least that He has turned His back or diverted His attention. We will face situations that seem to disprove God is in control—our natural reasoning would want to shout, "What God would allow this!" At times we will not see any divine purpose in the circumstances we are in. They may seem so evil, so chaotic, and so overwhelming that the suggestion of working together for our good seems almost like blasphemy.

To see how these truths actually operate, let's consider in more detail the life of Joseph. He was given several dreams clearly indicating someday he would be lord over his brothers. The circumstances that followed, however, appeared to totally disprove God's word to Joseph. Joseph's steps did not ascend from younger brother to ruler over Egypt. They were down, down, and still further down. His brothers' hatred increased. They threw him into a pit. They sold him as a slave. His social status went down, not up. Being in Egypt eliminated all contact with his family, let alone his ruling over them. He was falsely accused and thrown into prison. The likelihood of God's promises ever being fulfilled seemed less than zero.

At nearly any point along the downward way of Joseph's circumstances, his natural inclinations would have been against believing the truths we just considered.

1. God is.

2. God is sovereign.

3. God has eternal purposes for His people.

4. God is able to use bad circumstances to accomplish His good purposes in our lives.

5. God's purposes for us include producing from our lives a message of His power and grace.

6. God's purposes for us are higher than we can see. "Where is such a God?" Joseph might well have asked.

And yet, knowing the end of the story, we can come back to every one of these truths and affirm, "Yes, that is the truth, and Joseph's life confirms it."

How do we have faith?

Having looked at the importance of faith as an alternative to emotion-based responses of anger, we might ask, "But how do we have faith?" Knowing faith is important does not automatically bring a faith response.

The Scriptures indicate faith is not a static product one receives ready-made, finished, and forever settled; but rather, faith is a living, growing, dynamic quality. We have already seen from Hebrews 11:6 that faith is a MUST in coming to God. How much of a MUST it is, we may not fully appreciate until the reality of our salvation is complete.

In any case, the faith by which we receive Christ may be an undeveloped, immature little infant that squawks and whines and even makes messes. Jesus, in His infinite patience and love, wants to nurture that faith out of infancy, even beyond energetic childhood and impetuous youth, into a robust, healthy adult, able to work effectively in His kingdom.

So how does faith grow? Following are several ways given in the Bible:

1. *Faith grows out of exposure to the Word of God.* "So then faith cometh by hearing, and hearing by the word of God" (Romans 10:17). God has chosen to reveal Himself through His written Word. "He made known his ways unto Moses, his acts unto the children of Israel" (Psalm 103:7).

   In God's Word we are exposed to the character of God. The account of Creation reveals His power and majesty. His laws reveal His holiness and justice. Bible history reveals His sovereignty, His providence, His longsuffering and goodness. The Gospels reveal His compassion and love through His Son and His plan to redeem fallen and destitute humanity.

   In God's Word we are also exposed to the works of God. This God can make a universe out of nothing. He can part the sea, cause the sun to stand still, produce a flowing well out of a rock, rain down fire and hail, shut up the heavens so there is no rain, send hornets or lions or whales to do His will, set up kings, pull down nations, still storms, heal the sick, open prison doors, and raise the dead. "With God NOTH-ING shall be impossible" (Luke 1:37).

As we read in the Scripture about the works of God, our faith grows. We come to the assurance that God is able to intervene in any situation, and if He chooses not to, it is not due to lack of interest or ability on His part, but only because He has higher plans we cannot fully see. Instead of lashing out, growing frustrated, or allowing bitterness to set in, we can rest in the "everlasting arms" (Deuteronomy 33:27). We can plant our feet on the immovable Rock (Deuteronomy 32:4). We can "be still, and know" that He is God (Psalm 46:10). We can trust that "this God is our God for ever and ever: he will be our guide even unto death" (Psalm 48:14).

If we would grow in faith, we must make opportunities to expose our hearts to the Word of God.

a. *We must attend to the preaching of God's Word.* Those who would grow in faith need to be part of a church where God's Word is preached faithfully and clearly. Not only so, they should pray for their minister(s), pay attention during the sermon, and express encouragement to him afterwards. It helps to take notes. It helps even more to discuss the sermon afterwards with fellow believers.

b. *We must read and study God's Word ourselves.* Peter wrote, "As newborn babes, desire the sincere milk of the word, that ye may grow thereby" (1 Peter 2:2). For devotional reading of the Bible to be meaningful it should be systematic. Projects such as reading through a book, doing topical studies (such as a study of *meekness*), or doing a character study help us to be systematic in coming to the

Bible, rather than using a random approach. It helps to use pencil and paper, and record insights gained through reading and study. Systematic reading, however, should not lead to formality. Variation is helpful. The point is that faith needs regular exposure to God's Word to grow.

c. *We must have spiritual fellowship with other believers.* To grow in faith means actually to become increasingly God-conscious. As we learn to know God and His ways, His presence becomes central to what we think, how we decide, what we plan, how we face situations, and how we view people. God lives in us. His Word becomes the substance of our hearts. As we interact with others, then, God and His Word become a vital part of our interaction. This is spiritual fellowship. It is not simply a Sunday activity or formal meetings with other Christians. Rather, it comes to characterize our interaction with fellow believers. Spiritual fellowship—talking to others about what the Lord is doing in our lives, praising His goodness, sharing insights from His Word, encouraging one another, confessing our sins and shortcomings, and praying together—this kind of interaction is rich soil for faith to grow mature and strong.

d. *We must read Christian literature.* Some Christian writers explain God's Word, helping us grow in our understanding of God's ways. Others write the story of their own spiritual journey or that of others. Christian biographies can be excellent windows into the goodness and grace of God, expanding our awareness of Him and increasing our faith in His ability to work in behalf of those who trust in Him.

2. *Faith grows as we express it.* "If thou shalt confess with thy mouth the Lord Jesus, and shalt believe in thine heart that God hath raised him from the dead, thou shalt be saved" (Romans 10:9). This verse gives us two essentials for salvation: confession and faith. We will first explore what it means to confess with our mouths and then see how the two requirements are related.

The Greek word translated "confess" is made up of two word parts meaning "same" and "to speak or say." A literal rendering of the word parts would be "same say" or more understandably, "to say the same thing."

Jesus is Lord. That is truth no matter what men or women say. When we "same say," that Jesus is Lord, we are simply agreeing verbally with the truth, or as the Bible says, we are "confessing" that Jesus is Lord.

Confessing with the mouth that Jesus is Lord, when accompanied with faith in the heart, confirms the reality of salvation. The words of the mouth are stating the conviction of the heart. Apart from faith, the words would mean nothing and there is no salvation.

Looking at the Greek verbs more closely, we find they are in the form showing continuing action. God is calling for more than a one-time confession made upon receiving Christ as Saviour or at one's baptism. Rather, He is calling for ongoing verbal agreement with the truth of Jesus' lordship along with ongoing inner conviction of who He was, who He is, what He did, and what He shall do. "If thou shalt be confessing that Jesus is Lord, and shalt be believing in thine heart that God hath raised him from the dead ..."

Salvation is not dependent on some prayer in our dim or recent past, or on our raised hand at an evangelistic campaign, or on some words we said at our baptism, or on a faith we once had. God's saving work is the result of an ongoing confession with our mouths of our ongoing response of faith in the heart to the ongoing reality of Jesus' lordship.

What does confession with the mouth have to do with faith in the heart? Though verbal confession without faith means nothing, verbal confession with the mouth has a strengthening effect on faith in the heart.

Let's look at this specifically in the context of anger. One of the first indications of anger is what we say. If we manage to bite off the actual words, the words are flying inside our minds. When the initial storm subsides, distant thunder can rumble for hours, in inner mutterings, complainings, and accusations.

What is the effect of verbally expressing our anger and resentment? Verbal expression tends to confirm in our hearts the rightness of our resentful thoughts, deductions, and conclusions. The more we express it, the more we are convinced we are right, and the more settled we become in our view.

The same effect occurs in the Bible-based response of faith. Confessing with our mouths the lordship of Jesus confirms and strengthens and settles faith in our hearts. An ongoing and healthy faith, then, must regularly find verbal expression.

Difficult situations test our faith. We feel like lashing out or growing bitter. Instead of verbally venting our feelings, we need to be verbally expressing our faith. There are several ways we can do this.

a. We can express our faith directly to God specifically about the situation we are struggling with.

O Lord. I am facing a situation I do not understand. It seems overwhelming to me, and I see no good in it. My natural feelings are resentment, bitterness, and self-pity. But Your Word says that You are good, that You work in behalf of those who put their trust in You, and that You can work all things together for good to those who love You. I choose to believe Your Word. I do not know how You can do it, but I place my trust in You. I love You, Father, and I am willing to do whatever You ask me to do. You are over this situation. You are able to deliver me out of it, or You can give me grace to endure. I choose to trust You no matter what You allow in my life, for I know Your ways are right and Your character is totally trustworthy. I believe You are the same today as You were in the days of Moses, Daniel, and the Apostle Paul. You are good beyond description, powerful beyond measure, and wise beyond my comprehension. I am committed to You forever. Your child, _____.

It can help to actually write out an expression of faith describing the situation and one's specific feelings, and then, clearly and resolutely, expressing faith. It helps to read over this aloud on one's knees and to repeat it throughout the day. Ongoing confession with the mouth strengthens ongoing faith in the heart.

b. We can express our faith by reading appropriate expressions of faith found in the Bible. The Psalms particularly are filled with expressions of faith in God. "They that know thy name will put their trust in thee: for thou, LORD, hast not forsaken them that seek thee" (Psalm 9:10). "I will love thee, O LORD, my strength. The LORD is my rock, and my fortress, and my deliverer; my God, my strength, in whom I will trust; my buckler, and the horn of my salvation, and my high tower. I will call upon the LORD, who is worthy to be praised: so shall I be saved from mine enemies" (Psalm 18:1-3).

Many are the righteous who have found themselves sustained in difficult situations by reading from the Psalms. It is helpful to collect favorite expressions of faith, write them down, and keep them for ready reference. It is also helpful to read them aloud back to the God who inspired them. God's ear is especially sensitive to the sound of His own eternal Word.

c. A third way we can express our faith is to fellow believers. As we walk through difficulty in companionship with God, the Lord pulls back the curtain, allowing us to see more of Himself and of His ways. Sometimes we see only glimpses, and sometimes we are given panoramic views. But it is wise to talk to fellow believers about those insights into God.

As you think about difficulties you are facing, what is God showing you? What has He talked to you about? What blessings has He shared in the middle of your grief? your loss? your trial? your pain? your burden?

Job voiced his confusion and grief, and beyond that, his complaint that God seemed distant and unresponsive, even unfair. But Job likewise glimpsed God's glory and expressed his faith, though it was to friends who denied his sincerity. "For I know that my redeemer liveth, and that he shall stand at the latter day upon the earth: And though after my skin worms destroy this body, yet in my flesh shall I see God" (Job 19:25, 26).

Faith that is expressed grows. And a growing faith gives us a view totally different from the view based on our natural emotions. When our natural inclinations are anger, resentment, bitterness, and self-pity, how we need the eyes of faith in order to keep our focus on God! By faith we can come to view our problems through His wisdom, to view our needs in the light of His supply, and to view our hardships with an awareness of His strength.

Taking steps of faith does not mean denying reality. Faith does not make us immune to pain. It does not remove trial and difficulty. But taking steps of faith brings God into our situation. God not only gives us a different perspective, He also works in our behalf. Furthermore, the peace accompanying a response of faith is totally different from the emotional cauldron brought on by responses based on anger and bitterness.

Study Questions (Chapter Five)

1. Describe the two realms—the natural and the spiritual.

2. What is the place of faith in the spiritual realm?

3. List the six truths about God given in this chapter. These truths are important to focus on when we face situations that would naturally anger us. After listing each truth, tell how we are tempted to think when we become angry.

4. Different situations test our faith in different ways. Consider each of the following Bible characters and tell how he/she may have struggled with the above truths:
   a. Noah (in preaching to a corrupt society)
   b. Moses (in fleeing from Egypt as a young man)
   c. David (in fleeing from Saul)
   d. Jeremiah (in being persecuted for faithful prophecy)
   e. Esther (in seeing Haman's rise to power)
   f. Mary (in seeing her Son crucified)

5. Think of a difficult struggle you have experienced as a Christian (or a struggle faced by someone close to you).
   a. Describe the situation.
   b. How did the experience make you feel?
   c. In what ways did you act on your feelings?
   d. Which of the six truths about God did you find especially difficult to reconcile with the experience?
   e. Find several additional Scriptures that verify these truths.

6. Consider again each of the characters you looked at in Exercise #4. For each one, list several purposes God had in allowing the situation.

7. As you consider the experience you described in Exercise #5, what are some possible purposes God had in allowing it in your life?

8. Often God's purposes are beyond what we can see at the time. For each of the following situations, list God's immediate purpose(s), and then His higher purpose(s) that the people involved did not know at the time:
   a. God told Abraham to leave Haran and go to Canaan.
   b. God allowed Joseph to be taken to Egypt.
   c. God delivered the Israelites from Egypt.
   d. God caused the prince of the eunuchs to favor Daniel.
   e. God warned Joseph to leave Bethlehem.

9. Having studied these Bible examples, what additional truths about God can you see that are important to keep in focus when we face situations that would naturally make us feel angry?

10. List four ways we can open our hearts to the Word of God, and try to list several insights you have received through each means.

11. Which of these has been especially meaningful to you in your personal growth in faith?

12. Which of the four ways of receiving God's Word has been most neglected in your experience?

13. If you have read about the lives of the following Christians, tell how each of these people demonstrated faith and how through faith they avoided bitterness. (If you are not familiar with their lives, discuss this with believers who are.)
   a. Fanny Crosby (blinded through wrong medical treat-

ment as a baby)
   b. Elisabeth Elliot (husband martyred for his faith)
   c. Susanna Wesley (17 children, financial difficulties)
   d. George Blaurock (beaten and banished for his faith)
   e. Conrad Grebel (persecuted, imprisoned, and chased from place to place for his faith)
   f. John Bunyan (imprisoned for preaching)
   g. William Tyndale (persecuted for translating the Bible)
   h. Richard Wurmbrand (held in Communist prisons for preaching)

14. List three ways we can express our faith. Which of these have you personally found meaningful?

15. For each of the following Bible characters, find an expression of faith that is remarkable, considering his/her circumstances.
   a. Joseph
   b. David
   c. Job
   d. the three Hebrew boys
   e. Ruth
   f. Mary (mother of Jesus)

16. Think of an experience you have had that has caused you to struggle with anger or resentment. Using the example given in this chapter as a guide, write out your own expression of faith in God.

17. Using a concordance, find verses from the Psalms that express trust in the Lord. Write out several you particularly appreciate.

CHAPTER 6

THE RESPONSE OF FORGIVENESS

Unable to have children by birth, Cheryl and her husband opened their home to foster children. Later they decided to adopt two children who had become especially dear to them. In addition, they kept Karen, a twenty-six-year-old who was slightly impaired mentally.

One week before the adoption was final, they discovered Karen was pregnant. Then Cheryl learned the devastating news that her husband was the father of Karen's child. As a result, the adoption was stopped and the two children were taken away. Cheryl and her husband's relationship deteriorated until, three years later, he demanded that she leave.

As a Christian, Cheryl knew she needed to forgive. And she tried. But Cheryl got caught in a common misconception about forgiveness that actually kept her from truly forgiving. It is a trap we will explore further in this chapter on forgiveness.

Understanding what forgiveness is.

Jesus taught and practiced forgiveness. His teaching and His example help us understand how we are to forgive.

"Then said he unto the disciples, It is impossible but that offences will come: but woe unto him, through whom they come! It were better for him that a millstone were hanged about his neck, and he cast into the sea, than that he should offend one of these little ones. Take heed to yourselves: If thy brother trespass against thee, rebuke him; and if he repent, forgive him. And if he trespass against thee seven times in a day, and seven times in a day turn again to thee, saying, I repent; thou shalt forgive him. And the apostles said unto the Lord, Increase our faith" (Luke 17:1-5).

Several points come through clearly in this instruction:

1. *Everyone needs to forgive.* Jesus acknowledged offenses do come. An "offense" is literally a hurdle in another's path that can potentially cause stumbling; it is that which another trips over. It usually refers to something bad, but in some cases, the hurdle is the condition of the person who stumbles. Jesus, for example, was an offense to many of the Jews.

   Offenses are part of human experience. No one gets through life without facing experiences that act as hurdles, stumbling stones, barriers, even mountains.

2. *To cause another person to fall into sin is serious with God.* Although Jesus said offenses are sure to come, He did not say they don't matter. They do. "Woe unto him, through whom they come." We will return to the significance of this later, but let's recognize God takes special note of the person who offends.

3. *Forgiveness is for wrongs.* Jesus said, "If thy brother trespass against thee...." He is giving instructions for our response to actual wrongs. While this point may seem obvious, we often get caught objecting to forgiveness due to the wrongness of what the person has done. That is exactly the point. If the offense were small enough to overlook, we would not need to forgive. Forgiveness does not mean we are saying, "It doesn't matter."

4. *Forgiveness does not take away the need for rebuke.* From other teachings of Jesus and from His own example, we can assume Jesus is not here prescribing a step-by-step plan for dealing with every offense. He did not say we must always rebuke before forgiving, or that the offender must repent before we can forgive. Jesus Himself forgave at times without rebuking, without the offenders asking for forgiveness, without them even knowing they had sinned (Luke 23:34). But rebuke and repentance can be, and often are, steps in the forgiveness process.

This brings us to two important clarifications about forgiveness:

1. *Forgiveness must not be equated with denial.* This can happen in several ways. It was Cheryl's problem at the beginning of this chapter. Many people try to deal with extremely hurtful people in their lives by throwing their offenses in a "closet" in the back room of their mind.

    Sometimes they do this with the intent to forgive. The offense may have been the knife of unfaithfulness, the hammer mill of an abusive temper, or the emotionally crippling experience of sexual abuse. It is so painful that the mind goes numb trying to process what has happened or is continuing to happen. "Forgive!" the Bible says. The confused Christian believes to forgive means putting this terrible offense "out of mind." The offense is thrown into this back closet and the door is shut. "No more thinking about this! No more feeling this terrible pain! Forgive, forgive, forgive! I will go on and have nothing more to do with the feelings that scream from this experience."

    There are numerous problems with this approach to painful offenses. First, this is not forgiveness. It is denial.

True forgiveness allows us to look squarely at the wrong. Forgiveness does not mean "I approve." It is not saying, "It's all right." Any attempt to forgive that becomes denial actually impedes the forgiveness process. We cannot truly forgive what we refuse to look at.

Some realities in life are terribly difficult to look at in the face. But denial does not bring healing. It prolongs the agony of the offense by letting it remain in the heart under an assumed name. Instead of facing squarely the truth that "My husband has been unfaithful," it is saying, "My hubby probably didn't mean to," or "It's all in the past, and it's going to be all right."

Life has a way of jerking open our closet doors. Hubby is an hour late coming home from work...and all the accumulated pain and anger and terrible memories come tumbling out of the closet, making a mess all over the soul.

Denial NEVER brings true forgiveness. The longer denial goes on, the harder it is to clean out the closet. Patterns develop to cope with the stink in the closet. We train ourselves not to feel. We put up barriers to closeness. We learn to twist the past. All of these patterns have a negative effect on the way we relate to others.

The second clarification about forgiveness is related to the first.

2. *Forgiveness does not require that I forget.* We hear the old saying, "Forgive and forget." There is truth in the saying. As forgiveness takes place and healing sets in, the soreness leaves and only a scar remains. Forgiveness may lead to forgetting, but some scars never go away completely. Some offenses leave

permanent marks on the life. Physically, emotionally, and spiritually we may never be what we might have been.

But although forgiveness may not erase a memory, it affects how one remembers. After Joseph's father died, Joseph's brothers came to him asking him not to settle the score, and fearing he surely would. Joseph did not say, "I've forgotten all about that." He had not. But he looked at it now through the eyes of faith, remembering the mistreatment, but choosing to see that God had used their wickedness for His own good purposes. "Am I in the place of God?" Joseph asked. "But as for you, ye thought evil against me; but God meant it unto good, to bring to pass, as it is this day, to save much people alive" (Genesis 50:19, 20).

Forgiveness is not denial. Forgiveness does not require that I forget.

So what is forgiveness?

Forgiveness means release. In Matthew 18:23-35 Jesus told Peter a parable to explain forgiveness. In the story, one man owed his lord 10,000 talents. How that translates into our economic system is less important than realizing that the sum was unpayable. The man was indebted over his head, plus! Buried. Then he was forgiven. Released from all obligation to pay.

This man went out and collared another man who owed him 100 pence. In spite of the debtor's appeals for mercy, the forgiven man refused to forgive. He held the debtor liable to pay and refused to release him, even though it was likely within the debtor's power to pay up with a little time.

The difference between forgiving and not forgiving is this key—releasing. The offended one lays down the demand for a price from the one who has offended. The offended relinquishes the right to collar the offender, physically, verbally, mentally, and emotionally.

Of course, forgiveness takes place on the personal level only. The offended person is not in the place of God to forgive sins in the absolute sense. Whatever sins the offender has committed must still be reckoned with before God. That is, in fact, the very reason we are called to forgive on a personal level. "Dearly beloved, avenge not yourselves, but rather give place unto wrath: for it is written, Vengeance is mine; I will repay, saith the Lord" (Romans 12:19).

Understanding how to forgive.

Although forgiveness is a relatively simple matter to understand, it can be very difficult to practice. We will look at a number of pointers that make forgiveness not only possible, but meaningful. Let's start with the hardest one first.

1. *Forgiveness requires self-denial.* There are a number of factors that can make forgiveness difficult, but none is so significant as the one lying within us. When the Biblical teaching on forgiveness zeros in on the offenders in our lives, self raises immediate objection. Some objection is overt and angry. "No way will I forgive that person!" Some objection is covert and sly. "I simply can't" (making it sound as if I don't have a choice). Or "If you knew all I have gone through," as though keeping the injury in view relieves me from the obligation to forgive.

   Some people have oversimplified forgiveness by saying it is only a matter of choice. "All you have to do is choose to forgive," they say. That is simplistic. One may have a desire to forgive and still not know how actually to release. This is especially so if one has grown bitter and offenses have become one's security. Indeed, forgiveness does demand choice on the part of the forgiver. It will not happen apart from choosing to forgive. But choosing alone does not release from the bondage of bitterness. Forgiveness also requires death to self. Unfortunately, the ungrateful wretch in Jesus' parable lives in each of our hearts and must be reckoned with.

2. *Forgiveness requires faith in God.* The actual process of forgiving (personally releasing) the offender depends largely on where our focus is. As long as we are focusing on the offender—what he did and how it has affected our lives—we will have trouble forgiving. We may know the importance of forgiveness. We may desire to forgive. But our offender-conscious perspective makes forgiveness impossible. We may release the offender momentarily, but we cannot let him be. Five minutes after we have "released" him, we find ourselves again mentally reviewing his offenses, mentally creating conversations with him, mentally tallying, imagining, correcting, arguing . . . and winning.

True forgiveness demands that we change our focus from the offender to God. The offender-conscious view must be replaced with a God-conscious view. We must allow God to be the God He proclaims Himself to be in the Bible. He is God. He is the final Judge. He is able to work in behalf of those who trust Him. Although He does not approve of the evil in this world, He does permit it. Evil people, however, cannot frustrate His purposes in the lives of those who are trusting in Him.

Getting God in our focus does not so much change the situation as change our perspective of it. Instead of frustration at situations out of our control, we can have peace, knowing they are not out of God's control. Instead of resentment toward the people who have hurt us, we can have gratitude toward the God who can heal us and can actually use the very people who hurt us to bring about good effects in our lives. Instead of mentally reviewing what the offender has done, we can mentally review what God has done. Instead of imagining evil and expecting the worst in the offender, we can imagine what blessings God can bring out of it. We can begin to praise and thank the Lord in faith for the good He will bring.

Developing God-consciousness in place of offender-consciousness takes practice. We are not naturally inclined to do so. But the new nature of the believer responds to the God-conscious view. It leaps with joy to know such a God exists. He is not a fabrication of our imagination. He is the real God of the Bible.

We saw earlier that God considers offenses to be serious. Jesus said it would be better for an offender to be thrown into the sea with a millstone tied to his neck and drowned than to have his record stained with an offense. God is perfect in justice. He is the One (and only one) who sets matters absolutely straight. God-consciousness assures us we can trust retribution to Him. The sooner we turn the offender loose from our hands, the better, lest we in turn become offenders ourselves.

The God-conscious view makes forgiveness a privilege. When we see God for who He is, we gladly release the offender. When our eyes are seeing God as our Rock and Deliverer, we no longer desire to hang onto the offender with our teeth clenched, muttering,

"You can't do this to me." We have no desire to continue to carry the offender mentally with us to work, to the table, to church, and to bed when we can, instead, have the Lord with us. God-consciousness changes our attitude from sour to sweet, from accusation to gratitude, from frustration to trust.

As we develop God-consciousness, forgiveness becomes a pattern with us that replaces patterns of anger and bitterness. Like Jesus, we can view our lives in the Father's hands. People may oppose us, hurt us, even kill us; but they cannot destroy us. And all they do against us, the Father can turn into that which is for our good, for the good of others, and thus for the glory of God.

3. *Forgiveness exalts Christ.* The tie between our forgiveness to others and God's forgiveness to us is unmistakable in the New Testament. Jesus said, "If ye forgive men their trespasses, your heavenly Father will also forgive you: But if ye forgive not men their trespasses, neither will your Father forgive your trespasses" (Matthew 6:14, 15).

Why does God so insist on our forgiving others?

His reasons may be many, but the first one is clearly shown in the parable of the two debtors in Matthew 18. In light of how much we have been forgiven by the Father, unforgiveness on our part toward our fellowman is the height of ingratitude.

There is another reason God calls us to forgive, however—a reason that apparently lies heavy on the heart of God. As God's people forgive others on a personal level, they mirror the forgiveness available to all through the work of God's Son. By opening our hands to release the offender, we are giving him a taste of the mercy available to him at the cross. By acting in the interests of the offender even at personal sacrifice, we are demonstrating the heart of God as revealed in allowing His Son to die for mankind.

This view of forgiveness gives meaning and purpose to forgiveness far beyond the incidents at hand. We look deeper than what the offender has done, down into his heart, and we see a person needing the forgiveness and mercy of God. In this larger view we come to see we have a sober calling to portray Jesus to the offender. This may be the closest he will ever get to seeing Calvary, the nearest he has ever been to understanding the cost of redemption. We can show him by our own willingness to forgive injustice, by our quietness to accusation, by our own "intercession for the transgressor." We must do this humbly, not shoving our forgiveness under his nose, but quietly and brokenly in the pattern of the Saviour.

4. *Forgiveness requires that we clean out the "closet" of past hurts.* Some people hold grudges from long ago unrelated to their present problems except for one fact— these grudges stand as emotional barriers to forgiveness. Once we begin to bury our hurts in resentment and unforgiveness, there is no telling the extent of the emotional and spiritual damage we are in for. We may shut off truth in order to hang on to our ideas about the offender. We may shut off love in order to hang on to our right to be avenged. We may quench the Spirit's promptings, thus cutting off His inner instruction to us and stunting our spiritual growth. We may learn to erect protective barriers in relating to people. Without our realizing it, these protective barriers spread out in our lives and isolate us from people in ways we did not intend. The feelings locked

in a closet of unforgiveness are more wicked in their effects than anything others have done to us.

Forgiveness calls us to open the doors of our inner closet. We must face what really happened. We must look it squarely in the eyes. We must then face the emotions that went with the events—our hurt, our anger, our discouragement, our anxiety, our resentment, our helplessness, our shame—whatever is in the closet. We must finally face the destructive and wrong patterns we have allowed to hide behind our feelings. These patterns may include such things as subtle ways of altering the truth, possessiveness in friendship, self-pity, or control tactics.

Cleaning out our closet can take time. As one woman said who had been sexually abused as a child, "When I try to look at what is in my closet, my insides feel like they are frozen. Once in a while a chunk falls off, and I can look at it and cry." To people who have not experienced abuse, this kind of talk may sound strange. But once the door is opened, the process can begin. It takes courage. It takes honesty. It takes persistence. It may take a friend's help. But true forgiveness cannot take place if things are hidden away in that closet.

Study Questions (Chapter Six)

1. Through the centuries, God's children have often been mistreated. List specific injuries or injustices each of the following characters experienced:
   a. Moses (Numbers 16)
   b. Jephthah (Judges 11)
   c. Hannah (1 Samuel 1)
   d. Jonathan (1 Samuel 20)
   e. Tamar (2 Samuel 13)
   f. Elijah (1 Kings 19)
   g. Elisha (2 Kings 2)
   h. Jesus (Luke 23)
   i. Stephen (Acts 7)
   j. Paul (Acts 14)
   k. Philemon

2. Now for each of the above examples, tell what would be the natural emotional responses.

3. Which of the above people clearly demonstrated forgiveness? And in those cases, how did forgiveness affect the situation? How might these situations have turned out differently if the person had not forgiven?

4. According to Jesus' teaching in Luke 17:1-5, how do we know God considers offenses to be serious wrongs?

5. In your own words, explain how people actually deny injuries.

6. List some reasons people are tempted to deny painful reality.

7. What are the effects of denial?

8. Explain how forgiveness gives us a different way of remembering the same situation.

9. Read Joseph's words in Genesis 50:20. How would Joseph have remembered his brothers' sins if he had not forgiven them? And how do you think it would have affected his actions?

10. In interpersonal sins, forgiveness means release. What is released? What limits what we can forgive?

11. List some of the objections self raises when asked to forgive.

12. Explain how forgiveness toward others depends on faith in God.

13. List some of the characteristics of God-consciousness and tell how it changes our perspective.

14. Explain how forgiveness exalts Christ.

15. When we hold grudges, what are some of the damages that happen behind the doors of our inner "closet"?

16. In opening our inner closet, what are some of the things we need to face?

17. Make a list of people in your life you have had trouble forgiving. For each one, write what you need to forgive. As you consider the list, which steps in this chapter are especially important for you to take?

CHAPTER 7

THE RESPONSE OF LOVE

I met Bob on the streets of New York City. He told me his wife, Tammy, had married him against her mother's wishes. Tammy's mother wanted her to marry another man. After the marriage, the mother continued to work on Tammy, and eventually convinced her to get a divorce and marry the man her mother had wanted her to marry in the first place.

The divorce, the rejection, and the conniving embittered Bob severely; but through the pain and trouble, he was introduced to Jesus and eventually received Him as his Lord and Saviour. Bob began to grow spiritually. This is what he told me: "One day as I was praying, I suddenly realized the hatred and bitter feelings toward my wife were gone. I was actually praying for her." The light danced in Bob's eyes as he went on. "You know, some time later, I realized the hatred I had for my mother-in-law was gone too. I began to pray for her."

The transforming power of God's love is indescribable. It is that love we want to explore in this chapter—what it is like, and how it can become part of our response patterns in place of the emotion-based patterns of anger and bitterness.

Whom are we to love?

Our first answer may be that we are to love everyone.

Putting Off Anger

Many of us growing up in Christian homes have memorized that answer from childhood. But unfortunately in that generality, we miss some of the exact people we are instructed to love. Jesus was specific, and we will go now to some of His toughest instructions in all the New Testament.

"Ye have heard that it hath been said, Thou shalt love thy neighbour, and hate thine enemy. But I say unto you, Love your enemies, bless them that curse you, do good to them that hate you, and pray for them which despitefully use you, and persecute you" (Matthew 5:43, 44).

Love is a God-ordained response to people to whom our natural response would be anger. Specifically, when we feel like lashing out with angry words or actions or when we feel like holding grudges or seeking revenge, exactly then we are to show the love of God instead.

Let's examine specifically the people Jesus named who need our love:

1. *Your enemies: those who work against you and oppose you, whether openly or behind your back.* An enemy works against us. Jesus is saying the person who treats us as an enemy is the very one whom we should treat as our friend. Jesus is not talking about national enemies but personal enemies. He is not referring to foreigners we have never met, but the people in our daily round of living who work against us or treat us unkindly. Any person who says or does something that "arouses my fighting instincts" or "makes me mad" or causes me to become defensive needs my love instead.

   The most common enemies, by this definition, are hurtful family members, spiteful fellow workers, or carnal church members. Your enemy may be your spouse, your brother, your sister-in-law, your father-in-law, or your former best friend. But between you and

96

this person, trenches have been dug. Interaction with this person causes emotional bristles to rise on your heart.

2. *Them that curse: those whose words to you or about you are hurtful, including name-calling, sarcasm, accusation, condemnation, and belittling.* These are people in our lives who use words to hurt. Their words have all the effects of a curse—evil intent, harm, and destruction. By their words, these people make us miserable, hurt us, and hinder us in what we are doing. Again, Jesus is not speaking about people distant from us, but those with whom we interact in daily living.

   Destructive words include derogatory names. They include criticism and insult. Or they may be good words, but are delivered with carbide-cutting sarcasm. *"You are one wooonderful housekeeper!"* (When the house is a cluttered mess.) Destructive words may be "smart bombs" dropped by people who know our most vulnerable spots. Or they may be words that hurt in roundabout ways, comments we don't think about when we hear them, but make us sick as we mull over them later. Jesus said the people who wield destructive words against us need our love.

3. *Them that hate: those filled with ill will, contempt, unforgiveness, disdain, and dislike.* Hatred is an attitude. In itself, an attitude may not seem terribly destructive because its damage is not tangible. But those who have lived under the grind of hatred know what awful emotional pain it can bring. To know you are disdained, to read it in facial expressions and body language, to see it in the eyes glaring at you, and to live with this hatred daily is an unspeakable burden. These very people who hate us, Jesus said, are the ones who need our love.

4. *Them which despitefully use you: those who find pleasure in causing you pain or difficulty.* In this verse, Jesus has taught us our enemies include those whose words and attitudes are against us. Now He includes those whose actions are against us as well. Some people find delight in making others miserable. They find pleasure in cruelty. They get satisfaction out of seeing others suffer. Those are the people who need our love.

In the context, Jesus is speaking of being persecuted for His sake, mistreatment for living righteously. Not all injury against us is persecution. Some comes simply because we happen to be in the way. Some cursing and hatred and injury comes because we do wrong. If we bring on the hatred of others by carnal actions or words on our part, we need to repent and receive the consequences patiently (1 Peter 2:20).

Our concern in this study, however, is not so much the cause of mistreatment as the proper response: *Love your enemies.* Just what does this mean?

How do we love our enemies?

Now we will examine the specific responses Jesus gave.

1. *Love: Being committed to another's eternal good, wanting the absolute best for that person, and being willing to be an agent in bringing that about.* The Greek word Jesus used for love is a strong word. It does not refer primarily to the affections of a close relationship, but to a commitment that actually may ignore personal feelings. Enemies are not usually pleasant people to be around. Their very presence may kill affection. Jesus is not asking us to be emotionally close to porcupines

but to consider what is best for them, no matter how many barbs point our way. In some cases, that commitment may call us to stand back and wait. At other times it may call us to say or do something exactly contrary to the feelings churning inside us. Love will do everything with a view to what is best for the offender.

Jesus' remaining three pointers give practical ways to love our enemies.

2. *Bless: Using my words to bring goodwill, to bring hope and cheer, to encourage, to lighten dark times, to offer help.* "Death and life are in the power of the tongue" (Proverbs 18:21). Words of blessing are life-giving words. They cause the person who hears them to take courage, to have strength to go on. According to Jesus' teaching, it is those people who naturally would make us angry that we are called to bless. Their words have been words of death (cursing); ours in response are to be words of life.

This blessing needs to be timed appropriately—right words at the wrong time can have a negative effect. It is to be given with a pure heart—words of blessing given with a false humility will only gall those who curse us. Sometimes words of blessing may be given out of earshot of the one who cursed us, sometimes in his hearing but addressed to others, and sometimes directly to the one who cursed us.

Words of blessing may be in the form of a prayer, invoking God's favor on the other person's life. They may come in the form of a compliment, pointing out a good quality or an accomplishment well done. Or they may be simple courtesies such as, "Have a good day!" or "I hope your work goes well for you today." Words of blessing may give a sense of support: "I'll be praying for you today." However they come, these words should bring hope and healing.

3. *Do good: Seeing needs in another's everyday life and finding practical ways of meeting those needs.* People who hate us have normal human needs. Love looks at those needs as opportunities to demonstrate kindness and good-will in tangible form. The one who hates me needs to feel and see and taste love in response.

   Obviously, this takes discernment. The key to doing good is knowing what the needs are. If a man is building a house, dropping off a load of bricks at the building site will be doing good only if the man needs bricks. If he has no need for bricks, they will only be in his way. If a wife who hates her husband needs her kitchen drain unclogged, her husband may say, "I love you" ten times in a day with no effect. Her mind is only on plugged plumbing. To do good, we must see needs and be willing to use our resources to meet those needs.

4. *Pray: Bringing the needs I cannot meet to the Lord; pleading for the Lord's mercy and goodness upon another's life.* Those who mistreat us, who purposely do things to make us miserable have needs we cannot meet. Only God can change the heart. Jesus taught us that one way to love such people is to pray for them, to bring their needs to the Father in heaven. Those who use others despitefully usually have few friends. Often they are miserable people. And it is unlikely that anyone else is bringing their needs to God. We have the opportunity—and calling—to do that very thing.

   Every hurt can be a reminder to pray. Every injustice, every abusive name, every act of unkindness can be the signal to stand in behalf of our opponents before the throne of God.

In all of these responses, Jesus is our example. Jesus practiced what He taught. He demonstrated love, blessing, doing good, and praying for those who mistreated Him. The day He was used the worst by earthly men, He prayed, "Father, forgive them; for they know not what they do" (Luke 23:34).

Why are we to love those who naturally make us angry?

When Jesus taught us to love our enemies, He introduced the most powerful principle in human relationships. The longer we contemplate Jesus' instruction and the more we practice it in everyday living, the more we will see the wisdom of it. The effects of love are more far-reaching than we can know. Following are a few of the reasons we should love those who treat us badly:

1. *Love responses to our enemies will spare us from becoming like them.* Our natural tendency is to hate those who hate us, curse those who curse us, lash out at those who hurt us, and treat others as they have treated us—with a little extra for good measure. The startling truth is if we follow our natural inclinations, we will become like the ones we despise.

   If we allow anger to guide our responses, we will become hurters, haters, and abusers. We will descend into the very attitudes and actions that have been so difficult for us to accept in others. We may become even worse than the person we dislike most. Love interrupts this process and spares us from becoming like those who treat us ill.

2. *Love responses to our enemies will speed our recovery from their wounds.* When people say unkind things, do nasty

things, or have hateful attitudes toward us, it hurts. David spoke of men "whose teeth are spears and arrows, and their tongue a sharp sword" (Psalm 57:4). People can and do wound one another. When we respond in love, however, the wound can heal, sometimes surprisingly fast.

There is probably no better example in Scripture of love's healing power than that of Jesus and Judas. When Judas betrayed Jesus with a kiss, Jesus felt the hurt deep within Him. Here was a man who had received Jesus' call, walked with Him, heard His instructions, and participated in an effective spiritual ministry under divine anointing. Judas used his special connections with Jesus to gain 30 pieces of silver.

That hurt.

But Jesus responded to Judas with the greeting, "Friend . . . " (Matthew 26:50). The treachery of Judas could not stop the love of Jesus. As John testified, "Having loved his own which were in the world, he loved them unto the end" (John 13:1). Because of His love, Jesus could heal. The betrayal could hurt, but it could not destroy. In the long run, Judas hurt himself far worse than he ever hurt Jesus.

The opposite of this principle is also true. Angry, bitter responses to injuries only cause the wounds to fester and grow worse. Infection sets in and the injury refuses to heal.

Love responses are a balm to the suffering soul. From a human standpoint, we shrink from loving a hateful person because it makes us feel vulnerable to further hurt. That is true in one sense, but from heaven's standpoint, love strengthens us to receive hurt without being destroyed. It takes courage to love, but love is the best protection there is against permanent damage from our enemies. Those who love as Jesus loved cannot be destroyed. Victims of history's worst hate crimes who loved their enemies were never really victims in the end. They were conquerors. "Nay, in all these things we are more than conquerors through him that loved us" (Romans 8:37).

3. *Love responses to our enemies may be the means of leading them to salvation.* After teaching us to love our enemies, Jesus said, "That ye may be the children of your Father which is in heaven" (Matthew 5:45). Love to our enemies demonstrates God's love for sinners. Blessing them, doing good to them, and praying for them shows the sacrificial love God poured forth through His Son.

This surely is one of the higher purposes for loving our enemies. God is concerned not only about the effects of hatred on us, but the effect of our responses on our enemies. Love may be what brings them to their knees. Sometimes this takes time. Sometimes we may not see the results.

One day a hardened, angry Jew watched approvingly as an early Christian was stoned. As he guarded the clothes of those throwing the stones, he heard unbelievable words from the man being stoned, "Lord, lay not this sin to their charge" (Acts 7:60). The immediate effect was to further infuriate this Jewish zealot. He turned almost berserk in his mad pursuit of Christians. But when Saul met Jesus on the road to Damascus, he broke. And he broke completely.

To what extent was Saul's life-change due to the powerful message of love the day Stephen was stoned? In this life, we may never know. But this example shows us we cannot always judge the effect of love by our enemy's immediate reaction. Furthermore, those people who seem hardest may be closest to the kingdom. We are not called to judge those who hate us, but to love them. We simply do not know all that may be going on inside of them, nor the purposes God may have for them if they respond to His love.

By loving the most difficult people in our lives, we can become agents of God's redemption, ambassadors of heaven, representing the love that flows from a compassionate God to a wayward world.

4. *Love responses in conflicting family relationships will safeguard us from passing on negative family traits.* Much of the anger in our world today is expressed and received in the closeness of family structures. Even in Christian families there is far too much anger and hurt. In fact, probably the greatest hindrance to fathers in passing on their faith to their children is an uncontrolled temper. As the younger generation is hurt by the anger of the older generation, they accumulate their own simmering caldron that, in turn, boils over onto their own children.

One of the saddest ironies of our age is hurting children becoming hurtful adults. How can this vicious cycle be stopped? Mere determination is not enough. Children and young people may vow with clenched teeth, "I'll NEVER be like my parents!"

There is a law—we might call it the "law of negative focus." When a child resents his parents, he is setting himself up to reproduce the same characteristics in his own life that he detests in his parents. The harder he clenches his teeth, the more likely this process will take place. The principle is simply that we cannot cultivate positive character by focusing on negative character. Hate produces hate. Anger produces anger. Ill will produces ill will.

The only force strong enough to break the power of family anger is love. Love changes the negative focus to a positive focus. Love does not look primarily at what has been done, but what can be done. Love breaks the desire for revenge and replaces it with a desire for repentance. Love introduces compassion into one's view of parents, their sins, and the consequences. Love gives us freedom to fall on our knees in humility and deal with our own problems honestly. Love gives us a sensitivity to what we say, how we say it, when we say it, and where.

How families in our world today need the healing, cleansing, humbling effect of God's love!

The love God calls us to is beyond us. This love is "of God" (1 John 4:7). To have it requires us to humbly acknowledge our poverty and seek God's supply. To love when we feel angry takes us out of ourselves and into the heart of God. It actually means death to the self-life, death to the desire for revenge, death to resentment and ill will.

Furthermore, the love of God takes us on a journey. There is no knowing all the possibilities love opens up in our lives. When we love, God is at work every step of our way. We live like Jesus did—for the Father and for others. Life is no longer a series of troubles and difficulties that make us angry, resentful, and bitter. Instead it becomes rich with divine appointments. As we love, we are ever learning more of the Father's purposes, learning to think as He thinks, learning to see people as He sees them.

For the Christian, therefore, putting off anger is not an end in itself. We put off only that we may put on. We lay aside anger that we may take up the task of living and loving like Jesus. Paul summed it up well in his letter to the Colossian church:

"But now ye also put off all these; anger, wrath, malice, blasphemy, filthy communication out of your mouth. Put on therefore, as the elect of God, holy and beloved, bowels of mercies, kindness, humbleness of mind, meekness, longsuffering; forbearing one another, and forgiving one another, if any man have a quarrel against any: even as Christ forgave you, so also do ye. And above all these things put on charity, which is the bond of perfectness" (Colossians 3:8, 12-14).

Study Questions (Chapter Seven)

1. Jesus gave the teaching to love our enemies before He was rejected and crucified. List some of the people who became His enemies.

2. Consider each one you listed, and then tell why you think this person (or group) turned against Jesus.

3. Give specific examples of unkind words spoken against Jesus.

4. Describe the attitude against Jesus in each of the following examples:
   a. People of Nazareth, Luke 4:28-31
   b. Jews of Galilee, John 6:41, 42
   c. Scribes and Pharisees, John 8:1-6, 48
   d. Chief priests, John 11:47-53
   e. Jewish leaders, Luke 22:63-65
   f. Herod and his men, Luke 23:8-11

5. What hateful attitudes have you experienced?

6. What hateful attitudes have you had toward others (or struggle with having)?

7. List some of the ways Jesus showed love to those who mistreated Him.

8. Using a *Strong's Concordance* or other word study helps, define the word *love* as used in Matthew 5:44.

9. How is this love different from the normal love of humans (see Matthew 5:46, 47).

10. List some examples of the kinds of words that bless others.

11. In addition to the words themselves, what must we consider to assure that our words will be a blessing to others.

12. Give examples from your own life where the words and actions of others were very meaningful and helpful to you.

13. What attitudes must we have to be able to bless, do good, and pray for others effectively?

14. What are the effects of showing kindness and love to those who have ill will toward us? Does it always change them?

15. If we follow our natural impulses in responding to those who are angry and hateful, what will we do? In light of this, why is love so important in guiding our responses?

16. Explain how love responses speed our recovery from emotional and verbal wounds. How do angry responses hinder our recovery?

17. In this chapter Jesus' response to Judas' betrayal is given as an example of the healing effect of love. (Jesus healed from the wound of Judas' betrayal because Jesus did not resort to anger and bitterness.) What other examples of love's healing power can you give from the Bible or from history?

18. What examples can you give of love toward enemies that resulted in their conversion?

19. What often results when children are angry at their parents' shortcomings? Can you give examples of the "law of negative focus"?

20. What negative characteristics in your parents have you struggled with?

21. Based on the emphasis in this chapter, make a list of people in your life who stand particularly in need of your love. Beside each one, list possible ways you can specifically show the love of God.

Christian Light Publications, Inc., is a nonprofit, conservative Mennonite publishing company providing Christ-centered, Biblical literature including books, Gospel tracts, Sunday school materials, summer Bible school materials, and a full curriculum for Christian day schools and homeschools. Though produced primarily in English, some books, tracts, and school materials are also available in Spanish.

For more information about the ministry of CLP or its publications, or for spiritual help, please contact us at:

Christian Light Publications, Inc.
P. O. Box 1212
Harrisonburg, VA 22803-1212

Telephone—540-434-0768
Fax—540-433-8896
E-mail—info@clp.org
www.clp.org